LAND MATTERS

LAND MATTERS

Can Better Governance and Management of Scarcity Prevent a Looming Crisis in the Middle East and North Africa?

Anna Corsi and Harris Selod

WORLD BANK GROUP

Contents

FIGURES

MAPS

TABLES

Foreword

How can countries in the Middle East and North Africa ensure that their increasingly limited land is used efficiently and equitably for the benefit of present and future generations?

The authors of *Land Matters* answer this fundamental question. And in the process they detail the multiple challenges associated with poor land governance in the region, as well as the risks if these challenges are not resolved. In particular, the study provides insight into the legal and societal attitudes toward land, thereby shedding light on many other important development issues in the region—the rule of law, gender inequality, contestability and transparency, and the role of the state in land management—and how these issues can be harnessed to advance—or limit—social and economic development.

More specifically, this study examines afresh the ways in which the region has approached land management and governance. Drawing on new empirical work, the report identifies and assesses the many ways in which land and development intersect, particularly in the areas of agricultural productivity, urban development, social peace, food security, and water conservation. Examining the tangled knots of these issues, the report puts land front and center in the development dialogue, explaining the connections and offering policy makers a pragmatic framework to understand and address land issues. I invite academics and policy makers alike to review this important work carefully.

Land Matters also describes the ways in which entrenched legal, institutional, and governance challenges restrict access to land and its efficient use, exacerbating broader development challenges. The lack of effective legal and institutional frameworks for protecting land ownership and tenure security also magnifies social disparities in the region. In particular, legislative gaps often deprive women of their rights to land and property inheritance, resulting in the loss of assets that would provide financial stability for them and their children upon the death of a husband or male relative.

Even in the face of these challenges, *Land Matters* provides a constructive path forward. Going down this path will not be easy, however. The authors point to holistic approaches related to better management of public and private land—approaches that call for enhancing the role of the private sector, improving spatial planning and managed urban development, and harmonizing the legal and institutional frameworks arising from decades of political change, among other things. Development solutions take center stage in the report. Governments and development practitioners could consider these solutions for unlocking land for sustainable and inclusive growth. In fact, now is the time to openly discuss the options offered in this credibly researched study, especially because time is running short to confront the disastrous consequences of climate change. In general, land issues loom large in many public policy decisions, but they are not always explicitly acknowledged or examined.

Although land governance reform may not happen overnight, I am convinced it is critical to eradicating extreme poverty and boosting shared prosperity in the Middle East and North Africa. My hope is that the findings and ideas in *Land Matters* offer new impetus to address land challenges, while also emphasizing that the protection of land and property rights is achievable in all countries in the region. This report is a much-needed contribution to addressing a "problem that matters" to the citizens of the Middle East and North Africa.

Ferid Belhaj
Vice President for the Middle East and North Africa
The World Bank

Acknowledgments

This report was prepared by a team led by Anna Corsi and Harris Selod (principal authors) and comprising Myriam Ababsa, Amani Abou Harb, Meshal Alkhowaiter, Néjib Ayachi, Gnanaraj Chellaraj, Caleb Travis Johnson, Rafic Khouri, Eva Klaus, Siobhan Murray, Caglar Ozden, Javier Parada, Hogeun Park, and Souleymane Soumahoro (principal contributors). The team was under the guidance of Rabah Arezki, Roberta Gatti, Daniel Lederman, and Wael Zakout. Other contributors who provided data and ideas for the study reported here were Mahmoud Elgarf, Asif Islam, Mohamed Nada, David Sims, and Aradhya Sood. The gender and land pilot survey in the West Bank and Gaza was carried out by Alpha International. The Tunisian gender and land survey was funded by the Deutsche Gesellschaft für Internationale Zusammenarbeit (GIZ) as part of the ProSol program (Protection et Réhabilitation des Sols dégradés en Tunisie) under the supervision of Jenny Rust and Saadeddine Ben Ali. Data inputs were also received from the Jordan Department of Land and Surveys and the Saudi Ministry of Justice.

Since its inception, this report has benefited from the guidance of peer reviewers, including Gilles Duranton, Irina Klytchnikova, Paul Prettitore, and Forhad Shilpi, and from discussions with many experts inside and outside the World Bank: Imed Amira, Bochra Belhaj Hmida, Taoufiq Bennouna, Yosra Bouaziz, Nabil Chaherli, Ali Daoudi, Olivier Durand, Abderrahim Fraiji, Richard Gaynor, Richard Grover, Alison Hartnett, Adnan Ibrahim, Timur Kuran, Ghizlen Ouasbaa, Mohammad Sawafeen, and Annie Thompson. Valuable guidance and support were provided throughout by Issam Abousleiman, Jaafar Friaa, Jesko Hentschel, Saroj Jha, Ayat Soliman, Tony Verheijen, Sameh Wahba, and Marina Wes.

The team would also like to thank all participants in the following events at which the preliminary study results were presented: the Marrakesh Series Workshop, the Land Thematic Group, and the Geospatial and Land Global Solutions Group; the authors' presentation to the country directors; the regional consultation at the Second Arab Land Conference; the Tunisia country consultation; and a sounding board session at the School of Foreign Service at Georgetown University. The team is also grateful for discussions with staff of the UN-Habitat Global Land Tool Network and the International Land Coalition. Finally, the team would like to extend special thanks to the following individuals who facilitated the organization of some of the events or animated them: Sadok Ayari, Leila Chelaifa, Olivier Durand, Mohamed Ali Guerbouj, Olfa Limam, Piers Merrick, Anis Morai, Salim Rouhana, Eleonora Serpi, and Ombretta Tempra.

This report relies on data from multiple sources, including the *Doing Business 2020* database. *Doing Business* was discontinued by the World Bank in September 2021 due to certain irregularities that did not affect the data used in this report.

About the Authors and Contributors

AUTHORS

Anna Corsi is a senior land administration specialist with two decades of experience in land tenure and administration investment, policy lending, and analytical work in more than 20 countries across Latin America and the Caribbean, Sub-Saharan Africa, Europe and Central Asia, and the Middle East and North Africa. She has led policy dialogues in both middle-income and International Development Association countries, including in fragile contexts, while based in Washington, DC, and in Colombia and South Africa. She focuses on promoting good land governance and on providing land-related expertise in operations with strong land linkages. Before joining the World Bank, she worked at the Political and Environmental Affairs Committees of the Parliamentary Assembly of the Council of Europe in Strasbourg, France, on institutional reform and human rights issues in Eastern Europe. Earlier, she practiced law in Bologna, Italy. She holds an MA in international relations and environmental studies from Johns Hopkins University's School of Advanced International Studies.

Harris Selod is a senior economist with the Development Research Group of the World Bank. His research focuses on urban development, including issues related to transport and land use, as well as land tenure and land markets in low- and middle-income countries. His articles cover a variety of topics in urban and public economics and have appeared in leading academic journals such as the *American Economic Journal, Economic Journal, Journal of Applied Econometrics, Journal of Development Economics, Journal of Public Economics*, and *Journal of Urban Economics*. He co-organizes the annual World Bank Urbanization and Poverty Reduction Research Conference. At the World Bank, he has served as an invited visiting scholar, as a land policy expert seconded by the government of France, and as chair of the World Bank's Land Policy and Administration thematic group (2011–13). Prior to joining the World Bank in 2007, he was a researcher at the French National Institute for Agricultural Research and an associate professor at the Paris School of Economics. He holds a doctorate in economics from Sorbonne University, a BSc/MSc in statistics from École nationale de la statistique et de l'administration économique Paris (ENSAE Paris), and a BBA/MBA from École supérieure de commerce de Paris (ESCP).

CONTRIBUTORS

Myriam Ababsa is a social geographer affiliated with the French Institute for the Near East (Ifpo Amman). She is the author of *Raqqa : Territoires et pratiques sociales d'une ville syrienne* (Ifpo, 2009). She is also the coeditor of *Popular Housing and Urban Land Tenure in the Middle East* (Cairo University Press, 2012) and editor of the *Atlas of Jordan* (Ifpo, 2013). A former student at ENS Fontenay and Paris 1, she holds a doctorate from the University of Tours (France).

Amani Abou Harb works at the International Finance Corporation (IFC), where her work centers on generating new health and education projects for IFC. Prior to joining IFC, she worked in the office of the chief economist for the Middle East and North Africa (MENA) at the World Bank. There, she contributed to this report by conducting data analysis on gendered access to land in the MENA region. She holds a master's degree in public policy from the University of Chicago.

Meshal Alkhowaiter is a consultant to the MENA chief economist at the World Bank. Before joining the World Bank, he completed his master's degree in public policy at Georgetown University and worked with the Ministry of Labor and Social Development in Saudi Arabia for three years on various labor market topics such as youth and female unemployment. He is currently a first-year doctoral student at the London School of Economics, studying redistribution and economic policies across rentier states.

Néjib Ayachi is the founder of the Maghreb Center, a think tank based in Washington, DC, focusing on North Africa and political, economic, and security issues in the Sahel region. He has been a faculty member at George Mason University since 2015 and previously held teaching positions at the State Department's Foreign Service Institute and George Washington University. He holds master's and doctoral degrees in political science from Sorbonne University (France) and a bachelor's degree in English and American studies from the University of Paris 8.

Gnanaraj Chellaraj is a consultant to the World Bank. He has worked at the World Bank in different capacities and regions, focusing on cross-sectoral issues related to food and land issues, infrastructure, human development, international trade, and immigration. Between 2002 and 2005, he served as an adviser to the government of Singapore. He has a PhD in agricultural economics from Purdue University and an MPH (public health) from Harvard University.

Caleb Travis Johnson is a land administration specialist with the World Bank's Urban, Disaster Risk Management, Resilience, and Land Global Practice. He holds a BA in international relations and history from Houghton College and an MA in global affairs: governance and public management from George Mason University.

Rafic Khouri is a senior consultant on land governance, with a special interest in women's housing, land, and property rights in the Arab world. He is supporting the Global Land Tool Network's Arab Land Initiative and was elected co-lead of the Professional Cluster of the Global Land Tool Network (GLTN) Steering Committee in 2018 and 2020. He has been senior international officer of the Order of French Surveying Engineers. He holds a doctorate in development economics from Sorbonne University (France).

Eva Klaus is a research fellow at the Gender, Justice, and Security Hub in the Centre for Women, Peace, and Security at the London School of Economics and Political Science. She holds an MA in international economics and international development from the Johns Hopkins School of Advanced International Studies and a BA in economics and international studies from Johns Hopkins University.

Siobhan Murray is a technical specialist in the Geospatial Operational Support Team (GOST) of the World Bank's Development Data Group. She works with the Living Standards Measurement Study (LSMS-ISA) team to promote the use of global positioning systems and other georeferenced data in survey data analysis and dissemination and facilitates the integration of remote sensing and spatial data in support of a wide range of World Bank projects.

Caglar Ozden is a lead economist in the Research Group of the World Bank, codirector of the World Bank's 2023 *World Development Report* on international migration, and lead author of the recent flagship report *Moving for Prosperity: Global Migration and Labor Markets*. His research explores the nexus of integration of global labor markets, government policies, and economic development. He has edited three books and published in leading academic journals such as the *American Economic Review* and the *Economic Journal*. He holds a PhD in economics from Stanford University.

Javier Parada is a junior data scientist in the World Bank's Development Data Group. He is investigating advances in remote sensing that allow measurement of land use changes in fragile countries with satellite imagery. He holds a PhD in agricultural and resource economics from the University of California, Davis, where he developed an interest in international development, agricultural productivity, and geospatial analysis.

Hogeun Park is a junior professional officer in the World Bank's Urban, Disaster Risk Management, Resilience, and Land Global Practice. His work produces advanced analytics for complex urban challenges through a spatial lens. He has published widely in leading journals on urban planning and spatial analytics. He coauthored the World Bank flagship report *Pancakes to Pyramids: City Form to Promote Sustainable Growth*, and he has led spatial analytics for various knowledge products. Before joining the World Bank, he was a Big Pixel postdoctoral fellow at the University of California, San Diego.

Souleymane Soumahoro is an economist and research fellow at the Foundation for Studies and Research on International Development (FERDI). He has in-depth expertise in evidence-based research in economics and public policy. Using his background in economic analysis, research design, and policy evaluation, he has led and contributed to several World Bank flagship reports on economic development issues in the Sub-Saharan Africa, Latin America and the Caribbean, and Middle East regions. Souleymane holds a PhD in economics from the University of Oklahoma and a master's degree in international economics from the University of Auvergne Clermont-Ferrand (France).

Executive Summary

CHALLENGES

Across the Middle East and North Africa (MENA), land is scarce and immensely valuable because of strong geographic and climatic constraints (84 percent of land in the region is barren and only 3.5 percent is cultivated). The projected increase in the demand for land stemming from demographic trends, coupled with the shrinking supply of land arising from climatic and governance factors, are indicative of a looming crisis at a time the region is also facing a dramatic social and political transformation. The reserves for land cultivation are almost exhausted, and the room for expanding cropland under rainfed conditions is the lowest in the world, limited to only 9–17 percent of the existing area under cultivation, as opposed to 150 percent globally. Urbanization trends are also exerting pressure on land. With the urban population expected to increase by 60 percent (190 million) by 2050, under current conditions the total urban built-up area in the MENA region will likely have to expand by at least 50 percent (1.3 million additional hectares). And yet land remains inefficiently, inequitably, and unsustainably used.

Meanwhile, both firms and individuals face high barriers to accessing land, with adverse effects throughout the MENA region. Twenty-three percent of firms in the manufacturing and service sectors identify land accessibility as a major constraint on their business operations. Political connections are used to access land, which may result in the misallocation of land to politically connected firms instead of to more productive ones. In the MENA region, there are twice as many politically connected firms (5.9 percent) as in the Europe and Central Asia (ECA) region (2.4 percent), with a few countries experiencing very high levels of political connections among firms (up to 28 percent).

Barriers to accessing land reduce economic efficiency within and across sectors and perpetuate inequality, especially among women and vulnerable groups. Women in the MENA region have the lowest rate of ownership of agricultural properties in the world and are two to three times more likely to fear losing their property in the event of spousal death or divorce. Formal and informal institutions and gender-imbalanced social norms and practices (especially in rural areas and in matters of inheritance and asset management) do not sufficiently support women's rights. Indeed, women commonly face social pressures to "voluntarily" renounce their inheritance of properties—according to Jordanian *shari'a* court data, over the last decade up to a third of heirs fully relinquished their inheritance rights every year. Refugees also face difficult access to land, with conflict in the MENA region causing displacement of millions of people who lack housing, land, and property rights in both origin and destination countries. Moreover, the land scarcity crisis is exacerbated by conflicts, which are additional factors contributing to land degradation. In fact, a comparison of cropland areas in the vicinity of the Türkiye and Syrian Arab Republic border shows that the conflict caused the Syrian side to lose 7 percent of its cropland by 2017.

Scarcity of land and difficulty of access to land are worsened by poor land governance. In the MENA region, land governance systems are complex as they reflect the cumulation of regime changes and associated reforms throughout history. Legal frameworks are frequently outdated and not aligned with reality or the needs of the modern economy. In all but the rich countries in the region and Jordan, poor property registration remains a key problem, reflecting complex land tenure situations, onerous registration procedures, and a low perception of the benefits of registration. Furthermore, land governance policies are often poorly implemented because of institutional fragmentation at the central level and the weak reliability of land administration infrastructure, which complicates information sharing and coordination across central state institutions. It is not uncommon for countries in the region to have up to 10 institutions competing for responsibilities for state land management. Finally, in many MENA countries high levels of public land ownership, strong state control of the land sector, and centralized, opaque decision-making processes on the allocation of land outside market allocation principles have contributed to inefficient land use and facilitated elite capture and cronyism. According to the Bertelsmann Transformation Index country reports for 2020, in 16 of the 17 MENA countries covered, corruption, political interference, or cronyism affected property rights.

The lack of effective administration and allocation of property rights is compounded by distortive policies, especially those for agriculture. For example, water subsidies to agriculture incentivize unsustainable use of land and are very common practice in a region that spends 2 percent of its GDP on water subsidies—the highest level in the world. As for regulatory constraints, inadequate zoning regulations contribute to low densities, inefficient land consumption, and environmental harm. Poorly designed and improperly functioning property taxation systems do not encourage efficient land use. For example, several countries exempt vacant residential units from property taxation, which gives owners an incentive to maintain empty properties. Some cities in the region have large amounts of vacant land (in some, more than 75 percent of the footprint), leading a few countries to attempt to use fiscal instruments, such as a vacant land tax, to encourage the use of land for construction in urban centers.

The inefficient allocation of land and the heavy control by the state reduce the effectiveness of local economic development policies. For example, it is not uncommon for industrial zones to be established in locations with insufficient infrastructure and disconnected from labor markets. Weak land administration (registration and valuation) prevents the use of land as collateral, restricts the funds available for investment, and undermines the growth of credit and mortgage markets. For example, the percentage of households in the MENA region with an outstanding mortgage on their property (housing loan penetration) is only 9 percent, which is below the world average. The weakness of land administration, in particular the lack of recognition of tenure rights and costly and cumbersome formalization processes, combined with a limited formal land supply and poor urban planning, have contributed to the widespread informal housing and slums. Indeed, 24 percent of the urban population is currently living in slums, thereby perpetuating tenure insecurity, complicating dispute resolution, increasing the costs of service provision, and harming the surrounding environment.

If MENA countries are to avert the looming crisis stemming from land that is scarce, unequally accessed, and used unproductively, they need to urgently turn their attention to the land sector. This requires both focusing on sector-specific issues and realizing that forward-looking land policies are required to respond to the megatrends of high population growth and climate change and the aspiration for economic, political, and social transformation.

THE ROAD AHEAD

Modernizing Land Administration Systems

MENA countries should begin by prioritizing the modernization of land administration systems. Clear priorities for intervention are property registration, digitization of records, and improvements in transparency and the accessibility of land information.

Technology is important because of the scope for digital transformation in the region and the opportunities technology offers for cost-effective solutions, data generation and sharing, service delivery, and transparency, all of which are crucially lacking in the region. Updating legal frameworks to bring them in line with the needs of modern economies and reducing the complexities of land tenure regimes are long overdue. Complex institutional reforms are also needed to overcome land governance challenges. Steps should be taken to address institutional fragmentation and streamline land management functions, limit the excessive control of state actors, and improve transparency to root out cronyism. Land governance reforms, specifically those strengthening land taxation systems and public land management, could generate additional revenue and improve public finances. Functional land administration systems are needed to implement land value capture and support more efficient land use and land management decisions, particularly about public land. Land allocation processes should be more transparent and market-based to ensure that state land serves social, economic, and fiscal functions.

Considering Broader Policy Objectives

In addition to sector-specific interventions, MENA countries need to adopt a more holistic approach to the land sector. Governments should seek optimal land use to meet economic, social, and environmental sustainability objectives in the evolving context of climate change, population growth, and the many challenges facing economies in the region. Those challenges include unemployment, gender and economic inequality, and obsolescence of the resource rent model. Careful consideration will be needed of what governments can achieve and what is better left to markets.

Necessary trade-offs will ensue in terms of agricultural production and food sovereignty, water preservation, and urban expansion (for housing, commercial activities, and industrial development). Efforts to consolidate fragmented agricultural plots and move away from water-intensive crop varieties will be essential for hedging against cropland losses. A shift from the paradigm of self-sufficiency to be achieved at all costs to one of food availability and food security could also be needed to fulfill sustainability imperatives. Meanwhile, governments will have to prioritize more efficient urban land use through appropriate incentives and through the removal of institutional barriers that prevent the formal land supply from responding to the demand for land. This step will be all the more important because the region is facing phenomenal growth in its urban population. Finally, although the widespread use of land to fulfill the social contract in MENA countries may have laudable social objectives, it has resulted in land inefficiencies and appears to be an inefficient second-best approach to addressing the more fundamental problems of lack of economic redistribution and inclusion. Improving women's land and property rights will be an integral aspect of efforts to reduce poverty and economically empower women in the MENA region.

Acknowledging the Differences among Countries

Not all countries face land scarcity and land governance challenges with the same intensity, implying that not all proposed policy directions apply equally to all. Wealthy countries in the Gulf face severe land scarcity but have relatively good land administration. Although these countries still need to pursue their governance efforts (especially for transparency and public land management), they have to set clear directions (based on robust social, economic, and environmental analyses) for addressing strategic trade-offs about the use of their land. They should focus on removing adverse policy incentives that have led to inefficient and unsustainable use of the land (such as vacant urban land and water-intensive use of agricultural land). This will be a prerequisite for them to sustainably respond to the increase in demand for land fueled by population growth. Another group of countries—the Maghreb countries as well as the Islamic Republic of Iran, Iraq, and Syria—are more seriously challenged by their weak land governance, but they are less challenged by land scarcity than the first group. These countries will need to prioritize modernization of their land governance and administration systems. Only in this way can they have a viable land sector that supports growth and put in place policies that effectively address land sustainability and equity (including gender equity). For conflict-affected countries in this group, modernization of the land administration and improved governance will be key for the long-term viability of the reconstruction process. Finally, the third group of economies—Djibouti, the Arab Republic of Egypt, the West Bank and Gaza, and the Republic of Yemen—faces serious challenges in both governance and scarcity of land. For them, simultaneously improving land governance and addressing land scarcity issues are imperatives. Until land governance is improved, they will not be able to effectively address land scarcity (for example, knowledge of the land inventory is a prerequisite), adding more urgency to land sector modernization reforms. However, sweeping reforms, although needed, may be impractical. Gradual approaches are likely to be more feasible.

REFORM OF THE LAND SECTOR: A TOP PRIORITY

Because access to land and land rights are upstream of basically all economic activities, reforming the land sector should be a top priority for MENA countries. The scope for land policies needs to be comprehensive and account for market principles and economic and sustainability considerations. Although some countries have undeniably made progress in improving their land governance, clear paths to reform are still urgently needed. Nevertheless, important questions remain about the replicability of successful reform efforts across MENA countries because of their different political and social contexts. In addition, the involvement of civil society actors and a shift in social norms surrounding land and property rights will be an essential aspect of reform efforts. Addressing political economy bottlenecks and vested interests that have long prevented reforms is key to success. In a way, these issues are not specific to the land sector, but addressing them within the context of a particular sector could prove more feasible than a simultaneous effort in all sectors.

In summary, this report identifies and analyzes the economic, environmental, and social challenges associated with land in MENA countries, shedding light on policy options to address them. It places front and center the need for MENA countries to think about land more holistically and to reassess the strategic trade-offs involving land, while minimizing land distortions. It is directed at policy makers, land practitioners, civil society actors, and academics, aiming to inform the policy dialogue with state and nonstate actors so that MENA countries can better mobilize land for economic and social development. It is also an attempt to fill the major data gaps and promote a culture of open data, transparency, and inclusive dialogue on land that will benefit all stakeholders, stimulate accountability, and facilitate informed and evidence-based policy decisions. These important steps will contribute to renewing the social contract, accompany economic and digital transformation, and facilitate recovery and reconstruction in the region.

Abbreviations

BTI	Bertelsmann Transformation Index
CE	Common Era
CEDAW	Convention on the Elimination of All Forms of Discrimination Against Women
DID	difference-in-differences
FAO	Food and Agriculture Organization
GCC	Gulf Cooperation Council
GDP	gross domestic product
GIZ	Deutsche Gesellschaft für Internationale Zusammenarbeit
GRD	geographic regression discontinuity
HLP	housing, land, and property
IDP	internally displaced person
ISIS	Islamic State of Iraq and the Levant
MENA	Middle East and North Africa
MODIS	Moderate Resolution Imaging Spectroradiometer
NCPSLU	National Center for Planning State Land Uses (Arab Republic of Egypt)
OECD	Organisation for Economic Co-operation and Development
PPP	public-private partnership
REPD	Real Estate Publicity Department (Arab Republic of Egypt)
TFP	total factor productivity
UNDP	United Nations Development Programme
UNRWA	United Nations Relief and Works Agency for Palestine Refugees in the Near East
WBL	*Women, Business and the Law*

Glossary of Arabic Terms

fiqh	Jurisprudential interpretation of *shari'a* law
ifraz	Land subdivision
matruka/metruka	Public domain land in the Ottoman Land Code
mawat	"Dead" (unused) land considered state land by default
miri	State-owned land that carries *tasarruf*, which is the right to use, exploit, and dispose of land (*usufruct*)
mulk/melk	Privately owned land held in absolute ownership
musha'	Undivided common land (public land or customary held land)
shari'a	*Shari'a* or "path" is the set of practical rules about life and conduct in society, according to Islam.
Soulalyat	Women from Moroccan tribes who are asking for their land rights and proper compensation (*soulala* means blood link, tribe)
takharruj	Exclusion from inheritance (with a legal document signed)
takrim	Compensation, gift, or modest amount of money given to women
tapu/tapu senedi	Land registry (Ottoman Law)/title deed
tasarruf	Right to use, exploit, and dispose of land (*usufruct*)
'urf	Custom or local culture accepted in Islam as a source of local law (as long as it does not contradict *shari'a*)
'ushr	Tax on land (part of *zakat*)
usūl wa-fughūr	Close relatives (father, mother, wife, husband, brother, sister, children)
waqf	Endowment dedicated in perpetuity to religious (not necessarily Islamic) or charitable purposes
zakat	An annual tax that each Muslim is obligated to pay as a religious duty. The funds are used for charitable and religious purposes. In Islam, *zakat* is one of the five pillars of Islam and is considered a purification of one's wealth.
zemam	Boundaries of cultivated and uncultivated village agricultural lands in the Arab Republic of Egypt that are subject to agricultural land taxation

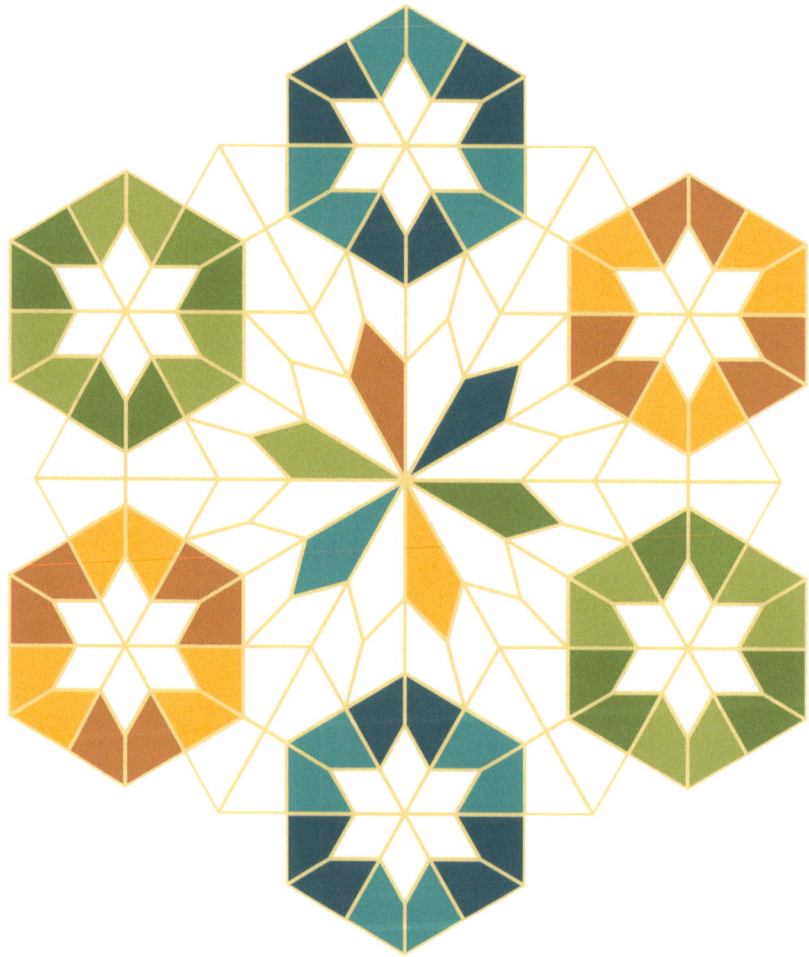

Introduction

INTRODUCTION

The Middle East and North Africa (MENA) region is undergoing a dramatic transformation from its growing exposure to climate change, water scarcity, strong demographic pressure, tapering of the oil and gas rent model, enormous social demands for reform in the wake of the Arab Spring demonstrations, and ongoing conflicts. These trends have increased the demand for land in the face of restricted supply and thus have implications for the ways in which land is used, accessed, and managed in the region. Improving the governance and management of land can play a significant role in addressing each of these challenges and putting the region on the path to recovery and growth.

The efficiency and sustainability of land use as well as the equity of access to land are central issues throughout the region. Three factors are in play. First, compared with other regions, in the MENA region the land suitable for agriculture, housing, and other activities is extremely scarce because of its largely desertic nature. This scarcity leads to competition among different land uses and dependence on the rest of the world for food production and food imports. Countries thus must make strategic trade-offs about the best use of the land to serve economic, social, sustainability, and sovereignty objectives. Underpinning these trade-offs are the objectives governments should legitimately be pursuing about the use of land and what would best be left to markets and comparative advantages.

Second, despite reforms in some countries, weak governance of land continues to hinder access to land, fails to create an enabling environment for investment, and prevents authorities from efficiently using land to generate revenue and to meet development goals.

Third, in MENA countries persistent economic and social inequalities affect the ways in which land is accessed and distributed. Women are particularly disadvantaged in the way they can access land and enforce their land rights. For example, unfair inheritance practices limit their economic opportunities and increase their vulnerability. Similarly, population displacement from conflict has major implications for land use and presents complex problems for efforts to protect refugees' housing, land, and property rights.

1

FRAMEWORK FOR A DISCUSSION OF LAND ISSUES

This report adopts a simple framework to discuss land issues in the MENA region (see figure I.1). The framework starts with the observation that two main constraints—scarcity of land and weak land governance—affect how land is used and accessed. Those constraints lead to inefficiencies and inequities, which, in turn, have economic and social costs. In this context, policies adopted by MENA countries both respond to and have an impact on those constraints, inefficiencies, and inequities.

With this framework in mind, this report identifies and analyzes the economic, environmental, and social impacts associated with the challenges faced by MENA countries in dealing with land. Although the report is based on in-depth research to shed more light on this situation, it is not an exhaustive analysis of all land-related issues in the MENA region, nor does it offer complete coverage of land issues in each country in the region. The audience for this report is policy makers, land practitioners, civil society, and academics with the goal of informing the policy dialogue with state and nonstate actors to help MENA countries better mobilize land for economic and social development.

In this report, state-of-the-art economic research is used to identify evidence-based ways to improve the productive allocation of land, to create gendered responses to inequitable access to land, and to respond to the land challenges stemming from climatic and conflict-induced population displacement. Addressing such challenges will require an approach beyond solving the technical land administration issues; it will also have to deal with constraints arising from inadequate legal frameworks, excessive control of state actors, lack of transparency, and cronyism, which could require major and complex institutional reforms. In a way, these issues are not specific to the land sector, but addressing them within the context of a particular sector could prove more feasible than a simultaneous effort in all sectors. Because access to land and land rights are upstream to basically all economic activities and have implications

Figure I.1 Conceptual framework for land issues, MENA

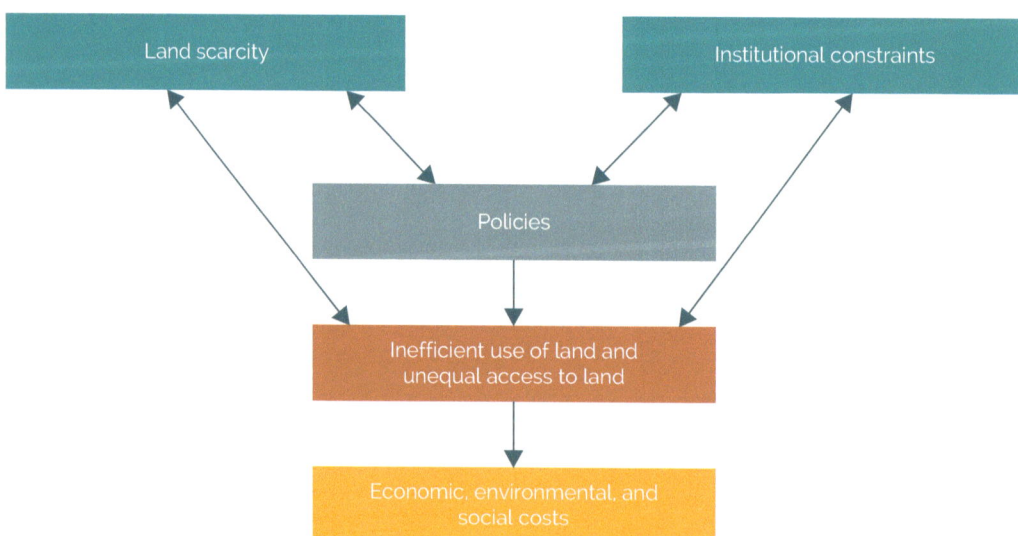

Source: World Bank.

for many other sectors (see figure I.2), reforming the land sector should be a priority in the MENA region. A major task will be filling the main data gaps and promoting a culture of open data on land that will benefit all stakeholders, stimulate accountability, and facilitate informed and evidence-based policy decisions. These efforts are important steps in renewing the social contract, fostering economic and digital transformation, and facilitating recovery and reconstruction in the region.

Figure I.2 Centrality of the land nexus

Jobs/ private sector development

Urban development (spatial expansion)

Inclusion of women and vulnerable groups (access to land)

Land

Housing (affordability, formal development)

Agriculture (productivity, food sovereignty)

Revenue generation (property taxation)

Financial sector (mortgages, credit)

Source: World Bank.

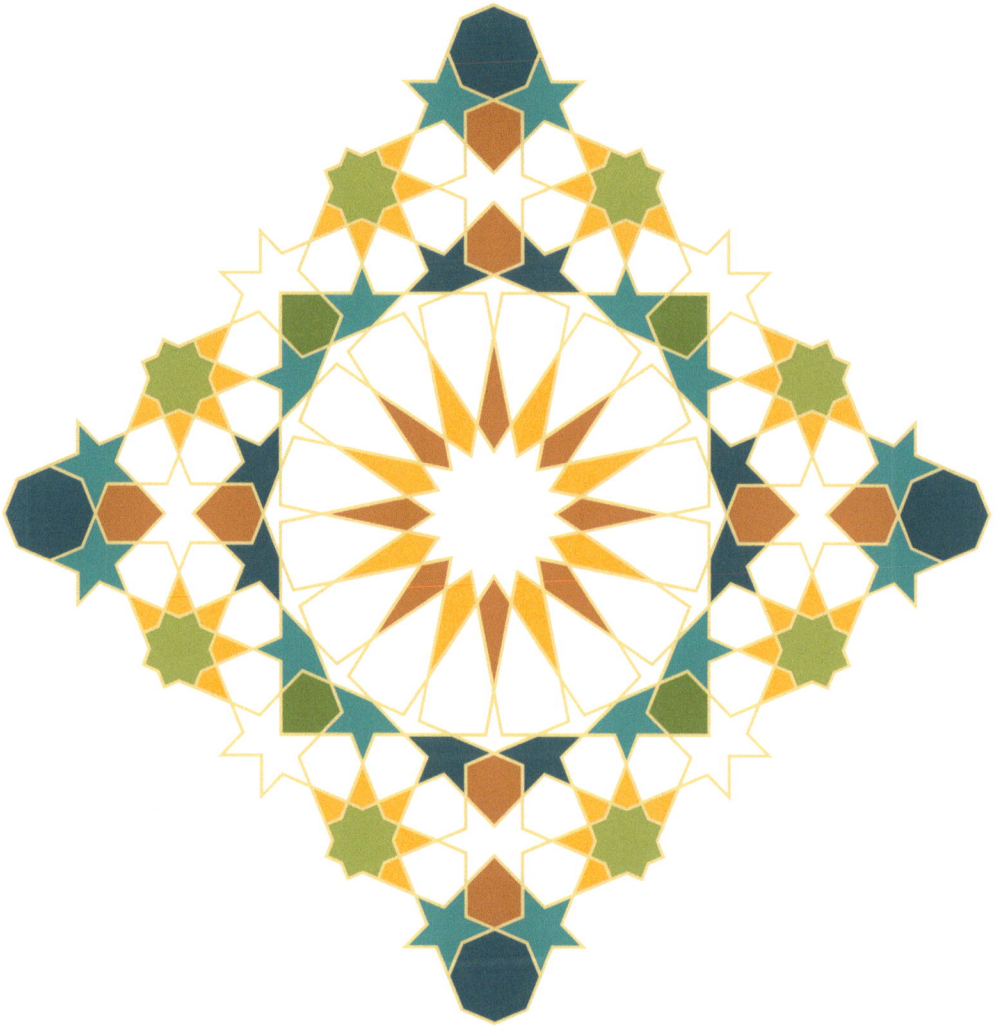

CHAPTER 1

Land Scarcity, Land Use Dynamics, and Land Use Issues in the MENA Region

INTRODUCTION

This chapter looks at land availability and use in the Middle East and North Africa (MENA), as well as the trade-offs among competing uses. It begins by introducing the land cover databases mobilized for this study before describing land use patterns, their determinants, and their evolution over time. The critical issue that emerges from the analysis is the severe scarcity of land in the MENA region. The demographic and climatic trends also analyzed indicate that the demand for land is increasing in the region, and yet land is under growing stress from climate change. Increasing land scarcity leads to strategic trade-offs about the best use of land to meet competing economic, social, sustainability, and sovereignty objectives.[1]

LAND USE IN THE MENA REGION: HISTORICAL TRENDS AND CURRENT SITUATION

For this study, both harmonized national-level statistics and satellite imagery were used to measure land use patterns. Measuring such patterns at scale is complex and requires building relevant indicators from diverse sources, including national statistics, modeled data, and, increasingly, direct measures from space. These data, however, are not free from problems. Issues may include lack of sufficiently detailed land use categories, limitation in spatial or temporal coverage, or insufficient accuracy and reliability.

To a large extent, this study mobilizes global data sets that allow for cross-regional and cross-country comparisons of aggregated land uses and for more detailed georeferenced analyses that rely on land use information about precisely identified locations. To determine land cover at a fine geographic scale, this study extensively uses the Moderate Resolution Imaging Spectroradiometer (MODIS) Land Cover Type data product constructed from satellite imagery available since 2001. Aggregate measures of agricultural land at the national level are based on MODIS Land Cover Type (henceforth MODIS MCD12Q1) as well as FAOSTAT, the time series database compiled by the United Nations Food and Agriculture Organization. Box 1.1 presents the characteristics of these two complementary data sets and describes their use in this study.

Box 1.1 FAOSTAT and MODIS Land Cover Type data sets

This study relies on land use data from FAOSTAT (http://www.fao.org/faostat/) and MODIS Land Cover Type (MCD12Q1) version 6 (https://lpdaac.usgs.gov/products/mcd12q1v006/).

The **FAOSTAT** database is available from the Food and Agriculture Organization (FAO) Land Use domain, currently for 1961–2018. Data are collected from FAO member states through the annual FAO Questionnaire on Land Use, Irrigation and Agricultural Practices. FAOSTAT provides nested definitions of land use. The large "agricultural land" category comprises both "land under permanent meadows and pastures" and "cropland." "Cropland" is, in turn, the sum of "land under permanent crops" and "arable land." The category "arable land" aggregates land under temporary crops, under temporary meadows and pastures, and with temporary fallow.

MODIS Land Cover Type data are a product derived from the Moderate Resolution Imaging Spectroradiometer (MODIS) Terra and Aqua reflectance data generated by two satellites that image the Earth every 1–20 days to measure large-scale global environmental dynamics at a moderate resolution (500 meters). This study uses annual data for the period 2001–19 from the MCD12Q1 product, which provides global land cover classes at the same 500-meter spatial resolution based on supervised classification of MODIS reflectance (Sulla-Menashe and Friedl 2018).

For simplicity of analysis in this study, land use types are reclassified into eight categories: (1) water bodies (at least 60 percent of area is covered by permanent water bodies); (2) forests (tree cover is greater than 60 percent); (3) shrub and grassland (is dominated by woody perennials and herbaceous annuals); (4) wetland (is permanently inundated land with 30–60 percent water cover and over 10 percent vegetated cover); (5) cropland (more than 60 percent of the pixel area is cultivated cropland); (6) cropland/natural vegetation mosaic (mosaic of small-scale cultivation and natural tree, shrub, or herbaceous vegetation, with small-scale cultivation covering 40–60 percent of the pixel area) referred to here as simply "cropland mosaic"; (7) urban (at least 30 percent is impervious surface area, including building materials, asphalt, and vehicles); and (8) nonvegetated/barren (at least 60 percent of area is nonvegetated barren—sand, rock, soil—or permanent snow and ice with less than 10 percent vegetation). Aggregated land use figures are obtained by summing up pixel areas under the MODIS cropland class (defined as having 60 percent or more of the pixel area identified as cultivated) and under the MODIS cropland mosaic class (defined as having between 40 and 60 percent of the pixel area identified as cultivated). Cropland mosaics are often located at the fringe of cropland pixels. In the Middle East and North Africa (MENA) region, however, the cropland mosaic class is almost negligible because its area is equivalent to less than 0.4 percent of the total area for land identified as cropland.

(box continues on next page)

The MENA region stands out starkly from the rest of the world because it is largely made up of barren land. The breakdown of land cover by category in the MODIS Land Cover product (figure 1.1) reveals that over 84 percent of the land area in the region qualifies as desert, whereas only 3.5 percent of the land area is cropland, and only 0.3 percent is built. Water bodies (0.3 percent) and forests (0.2 percent) are almost inexistent in the region. There are, however, large variations in land cover within the region. The country with the most vegetation is Lebanon (only 1 percent of Lebanon's land is barren), and more than 90 percent of the land cover of eight countries is classified as barren (Algeria, the Arab Republic of Egypt, Kuwait, Libya, Oman, Qatar, Saudi Arabia, and the United Arab Emirates).

Figure 1.1 Land cover breakdown, by region

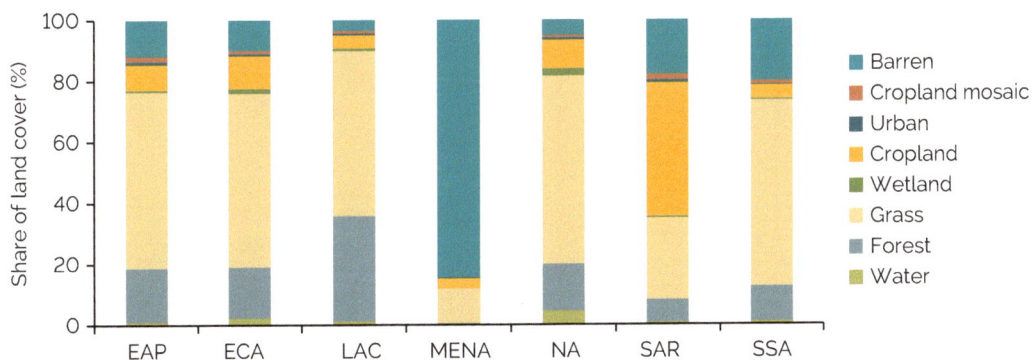

Sources: Authors' calculations, based on Sulla-Menashe and Friedl (2018) and MODIS Land Cover Type (MCD12Q1) version 6, https://lpdaac.usgs.gov/products/mcd12q1v006/.
Note: The regional breakdown corresponds to World Bank definitions. EAP = East Asia and Pacific; ECA = Europe and Central Asia; LAC = Latin America and the Caribbean; MENA = Middle East and North Africa; NA = North America; SAR = South Asia; SSA = Sub-Saharan Africa.

The suitability of land for agriculture is strongly constrained by geography and climate. The MENA region has the lowest cropland per capita and very little margin for expansion. Figure 1.2 (panel a), which aggregates FAOSTAT national data on land use at the regional level, confirms that the MENA region, with its 62 million hectares of cropland, has the smallest area of cropland globally. Of that total, 10 million hectares are devoted to permanent crops, and 52 million hectares are arable land (see box 1.1 for definitions).

This scarcity is compounded by the unbalanced ratio between cropland and the population of the region. Although according to these measures the MENA region has 4 percent of the world's cropland, it is home to 6 percent of the world's population. In share of cropland per capita (figure 1.2, panel b), the MENA region is at the bottom of the distribution, only slightly above South Asia and East Asia and Pacific. Cropland per capita (0.14 hectares) is only two-thirds of the world average (0.20 hectares) and one-fourth of North America's average (0.54 hectares).

Figure 1.3 (panel a) shows alternative measures of cropland measured directly from space using the MODIS data set. Although FAOSTAT and MODIS figures differ because of variation in what is considered cropland and in the nature of the data (see box 1.1), the MODIS data paint a rather similar picture, confirming that the MENA region is at the bottom of the distribution with only 38 million hectares of cropland. When measured from space, MENA appears to be the only region where cropland per capita does not even reach 0.1 hectare per capita on average (figure 1.3, panel b). Figure 1.4, which presents the distribution of cropland and cropland per capita in the region based on the MODIS data, reveals that there are, however, significant variations across countries. The Mediterranean countries, which enjoy a more favorable climate along their coasts, are more land-rich per capita than the Gulf countries, which are characterized by a more arid climate. In the Fertile Crescent, even a country such as the Islamic Republic of Iran that has large areas under cultivation does not have much cropland per capita in view of its large population. In fact, the most land-rich per capita countries in the MENA region—Morocco, the Syrian Arab Republic, and Tunisia—have cropland per capita that is only about 40 percent of that in North America.

Figure 1.2 **Area under permanent crops and arable land and cropland area per capita, by region, 2018 (FAOSTAT)**

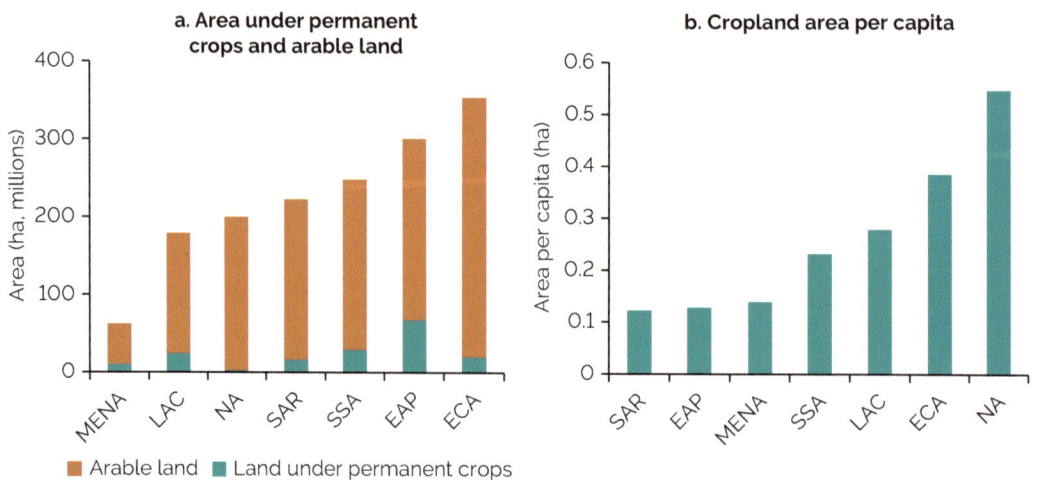

Source: Authors' calculations, based on Food and Agriculture Organization, FAOSTAT (dashboard), http://www.fao.org/faostat/.
Note: EAP = East Asia and Pacific; ECA = Europe and Central Asia; LAC = Latin America and the Caribbean; MENA = Middle East and North Africa; NA = North America; SAR = South Asia; SSA = Sub-Saharan Africa; ha = hectares.

Figure 1.3 Cropland and cropland mosaic, by region, 2018 (MODIS)

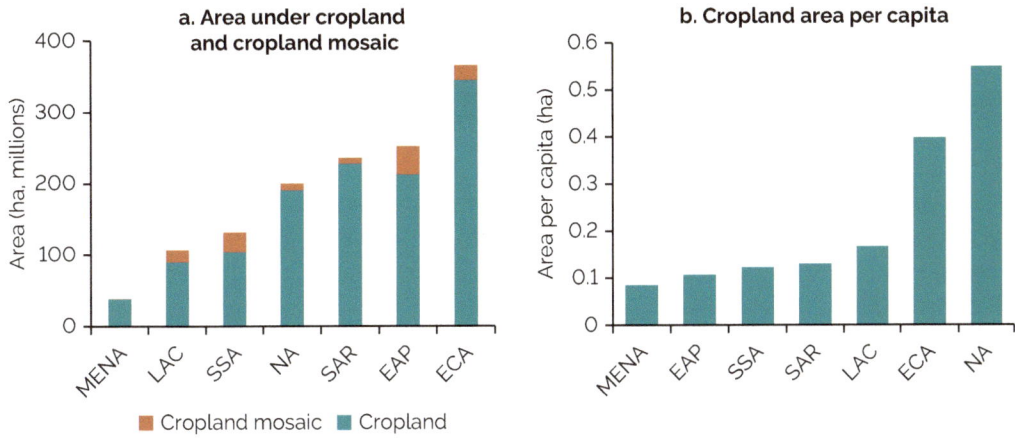

a. Area under cropland and cropland mosaic

b. Cropland area per capita

Cropland mosaic ■ Cropland

Source: Authors' calculations, based on MODIS Land Cover Type (MCD12Q1) version 6, https://lpdaac.usgs.gov/products/mcd12q1v006/.
Note: EAP = East Asia and Pacific; ECA = Europe and Central Asia; LAC = Latin America and the Caribbean; MENA = Middle East and North Africa; NA = North America; SAR = South Asia; SSA = Sub-Saharan Africa; ha = hectares.

Figure 1.4 Cropland and cropland mosaic, MENA, 2018 (MODIS)

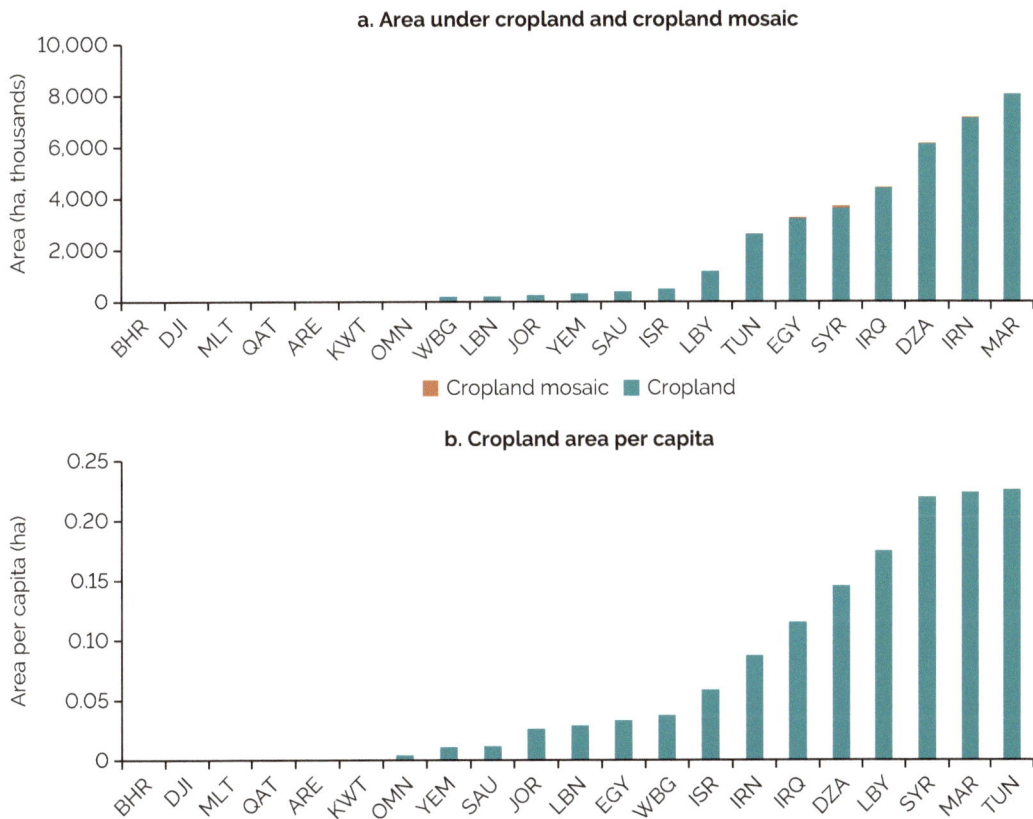

a. Area under cropland and cropland mosaic

Cropland mosaic ■ Cropland

b. Cropland area per capita

Source: Authors' calculations, based on MODIS Land Cover Type (MCD12Q1) version 6, https://lpdaac.usgs.gov/products/mcd12q1v006/.
Note: ARE = United Arab Emirates; BHR = Bahrain; DJI = Djibouti; DZA = Algeria; EGY = Arab Republic of Egypt; IRN = Islamic Republic of Iran; IRQ = Iraq; ISR = Israel; JOR = Jordan; KWT = Kuwait; LBN = Lebanon; LBY = Libya; MAR = Morocco; MLT = Malta; OMN = Oman; QAT = Qatar; SAU = Saudi Arabia; SYR = Syrian Arab Republic; TUN = Tunisia; WBG = West Bank and Gaza; YEM = Republic of Yemen; ha = hectares.

The scarcity of cropland reflects the agroecological limitations for expansion, and, overall, there is very little margin in the MENA region to expand land under cultivation without further depleting water. This situation is captured by estimates of how much of the current grassland could be converted to rainfed agriculture, which can be calculated by overlaying georeferenced information on land suitability with land cover data (see the methodology in annex 1A). Although this is a coarse indicator, it provides a fair indication of the limits to agricultural expansion in the region. As indicated in annex table 1A.1, under a high input scenario for agricultural production, the total amount of grassland suitable to grow at least one of seven major international crops in MENA countries without resorting to irrigation is equivalent to less than 10 percent of the current total amount of cropland in the region (compared with 150 percent globally). To cultivate at least one of the 27 major crops already cultivated in the region without irrigation, cropland could expand by no more than 17 percent. The potential for increased agricultural production in the region is thus seriously limited because its land is to a large extent degraded, and intensification at scale is also not a sustainable option.

Worldwide, MENA is by far the region most exposed to drought. Figure 1.5 shows the distribution of cropland area by exposure to drought for all regions (panel a) and for the MENA region (panel b). This distribution was obtained by overlaying current cropland locations with satellite imagery measures of drought over 15 years. The median exposure to severe drought over the period is 55 months. Cropland in the MENA region is therefore exposed to severe drought conditions 30 percent of the time or for four months each year on average. Combined with the volatility of temperature fluctuations and rainfall amounts, drought is a severe constraint that accelerates the pace of land degradation (IPCC 2019).

The MENA region is losing cropland at the fastest pace of all regions. Tracking the dynamics of land cover change globally shows that the mass of cultivated land is far from static, with some areas gaining and others losing cropland. Analysis of satellite imagery from 2003–18 reveals that all regions of the world experienced significant levels of gains and losses over the period (table 1.1), but the gross rate of cropland loss was not highest in the MENA region despite climate change and salinization. This finding may reflect the efforts by

Figure 1.5 Cropland exposure to drought, by all regions and MENA region, 2003–18

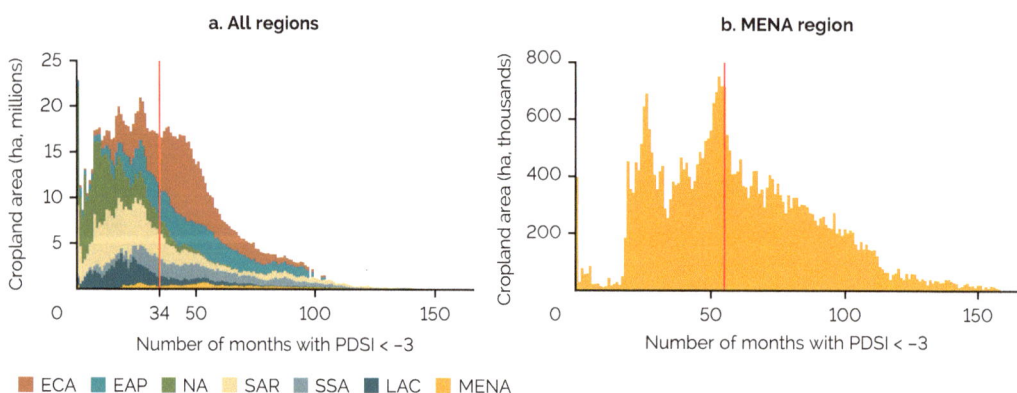

Sources: Climatology Lab, TERRACLIMATE, https://www.climatologylab.org/terraclimate.html; MODIS Land Cover Type (MCD12Q1) version 6, https://lpdaac.usgs.gov/products/mcd12q1v006/.
Note: These figures show the distribution of cropland areas by number of drought months during the period 2003–18 for world regions (panel a) and for the MENA region (panel b). Crop locations are identified with MODIS data at a resolution of 500 × 500 meters. Geographic information on droughts, defined as the number of months for which the Palmer Drought Severity Index (PDSI) was below −3, is recovered from TERRACLIMATE (Climatology Lab, https://www.climatologylab.org/terraclimate.html). The vertical red line shows the median number of droughts for 2018 cropland. EAP = East Asia and Pacific; ECA = Europe and Central Asia; LAC = Latin America and the Caribbean; MENA = Middle East and North Africa; NA = North America; SAR = South Asia; SSA = Sub-Saharan Africa; ha = hectares.

MENA countries to maintain cultivated land (in particular, though irrigation schemes). As for gains in cropland, the noticeable feature is that the MENA region has the highest share of new cropland gained from locations that were previously classified as barren, which likely reflects the desert land reclamation commonly practiced in the region. Although the net result of these dynamics was an overall gain in cropland in some regions (Latin America, South Asia, and North America), all other regions experienced a net loss, with the MENA region losing cropland overall at the fastest pace (−2.4 percent for the period, or −0.17 percent annually).

Urban footprints have grown quickly in the MENA region, often at the expense of already scarce cropland. Although the built-up area represents only 0.2 percent of land cover, it has grown significantly over the last decades. MODIS data indicate a 10 percent increase in the urban-built area over the 2003–18 period, which is significantly less than in Asia and Sub-Saharan Africa but significantly more than in other regions.[2] In MENA countries, cities often expand into the prime agricultural land surrounding cities. According to satellite imagery, over the last 15 years 24 percent of spatial urban growth in the region occurred on land that was previously cropped (see figure 1.6, panel a). For some economies, the figure for urban expansion into cropland is even much higher: 39 percent in the West Bank and Gaza, 43 percent in Syria, and 47 percent in Egypt over the same 15-year period.[3] For the region as a whole, this represents destruction of only 0.1 percent of the total cropland mass (figure 1.6, panel b), but more than 0.9 percent of the cropland mass in Egypt and 1.8 percent in the West Bank and Gaza were lost to urban growth. In this context, whether the conversion of agricultural land to urban land should be discouraged rather than left to markets is an important policy question, which is further discussed in this report.

Table 1.1 Movements in and out of cropland, by region, 2003–18

Cropland gains and losses	EAP	ECA	LAC	MENA	NA	SAR	SSA
Percentage change in cropland	−2.0	−2.3	14.3	−2.4	0.4	2.3	−1.3
Percentage of 2003 cropland lost	11.7	8.9	13.8	11	6.5	4.5	20.3
Percentage of 2018 cropland gained (from barren land)	10.57 (0.00)	6.9 (0.00)	23.8 (0.01)	9 (0.23)	6.94 (0.00)	6.9 (0.05)	19.29 (0.00)

Source: Authors' calculations, based on Sulla-Menashe and Friedl (2018); MODIS Land Cover Type (MCD12Q1) version 6, https://lpdaac.usgs.gov/products/mcd12q1v006/.
Note: EAP = East Asia and Pacific; ECA = Europe and Central Asia; LAC = Latin America and the Caribbean; MENA = Middle East and North Africa; NA = North America; SAR = South Asia; SSA = Sub-Saharan Africa.

Figure 1.6 Land use conversion, MENA, 2003–18

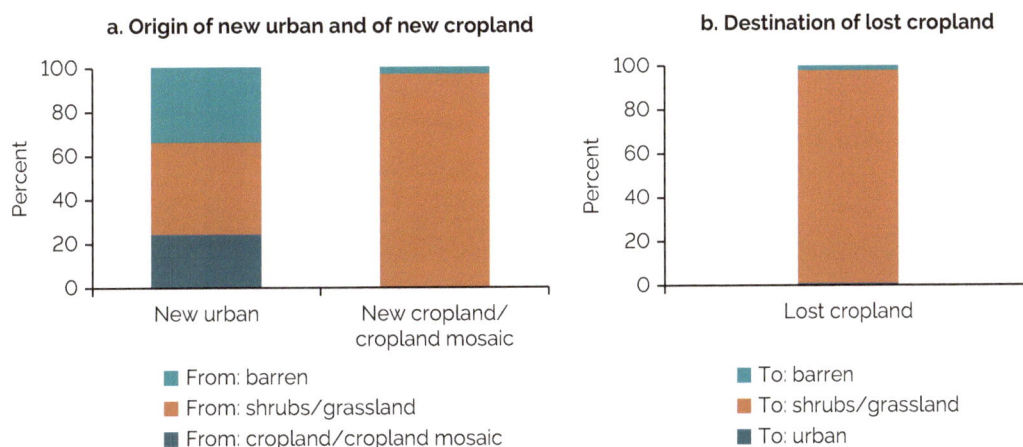

a. Origin of new urban and of new cropland

From: barren
From: shrubs/grassland
From: cropland/cropland mosaic

b. Destination of lost cropland

To: barren
To: shrubs/grassland
To: urban

Source: Authors' calculations, based on MODIS Land Cover Type (MCD12Q1) version 6, https://lpdaac.usgs.gov/products/mcd12q1v006/.

KEY DRIVERS OF LAND USE PATTERNS IN MENA COUNTRIES

This section assesses the key drivers of land use—demography, climate, institutions, and conflict[4]—for cities and agriculture in the MENA region. Generally, natural endowments have a large influence on where people live and where economic activities take place, especially in arid regions. A quick look at a map reveals that in MENA countries cities and agriculture are mostly located along the coastline and near rivers. These areas are more attractive because of their more favorable climate, land more suitable for cultivation, and better accessibility for trade. However, land use patterns can change over time in response to the changing needs of economies and evolving contexts.

Urban population growth in the MENA region has resulted in urban expansion like elsewhere in the world. In the region, the urban built-up area has been steadily increasing in response to its urban population growth of 2.5 percent a year over the last two decades.[5] But cities in the region have responded by using land less efficiently, with large cities experiencing decreases in densities. To quantify the land use implications of urban population growth, UN-Habitat's urban indicator database (UN-Habitat 2018) was used to plot land consumption rates against population growth rates for the period 2000–2015 (figure 1.7).

Figure 1.7 Growth in land consumption and urban population, MENA and rest of the world, 2000–2015

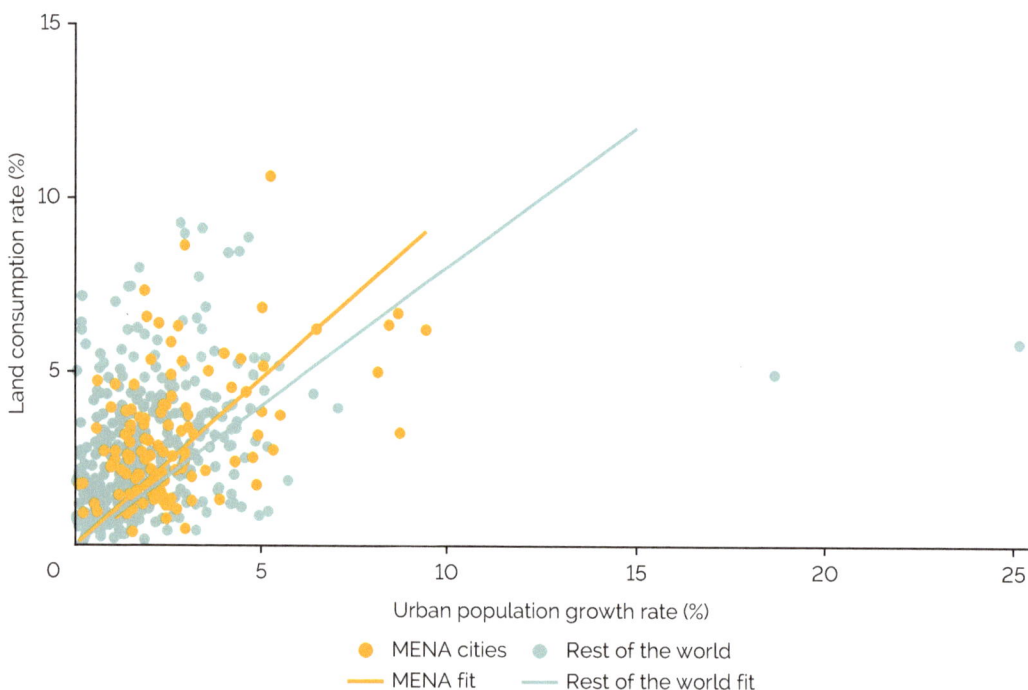

Source: Authors' calculations, based on UN-Habitat (2018).
Note: The figure distinguishes between cities located in the MENA region (yellow dots) and cities in the rest of the world (grey dots). The land consumption rate is defined as $ln(Urb_{t+1}/Urb_t)/y$, where Urb_{t+1} and Urb_t are the total area of the urban extent in the current year and in the initial year, respectively, and y is the number of years between the two measures. Similarly, urban population growth is defined as $ln(Pop_{t+1}/Pop_t)/y$. The data are available for 581 cities. Another slightly larger data set is available from UN-Habitat for the same period, but only with the ratio of these two rates, not the rates themselves.

A simple statistical analysis shows a built-up elasticity of population of 0.93 percent—in other words, a 10 percent increase in population goes along with a 9.3 percent expansion of the urban footprint. Thus a 10 percent increase in the population of a hypothetical city of 100,000 hectares will require the conversion of 9,300 hectares to built-up area. Interestingly, the elasticity for MENA cities is greater than the rest of the world by almost 14 percent, implying that, on average, MENA cities respond less efficiently than other cities in the world to a demand for space. This is consistent with the findings of a recent World Bank study revealing that MENA cities tend to grow in a fragmented, sprawling way (World Bank 2020). Analysis of a complementary data set of urban populations and footprints built by Blankespoor, Khan, and Selod (2017) found that larger cities in the MENA region (those with 300,000 or more inhabitants) are even less efficient than smaller cities, with an estimated elasticity of 1.15, compared with 0.73 for smaller cities in the region.[6] An elasticity greater than 1 indicates a tendency of larger MENA cities to see overall decreasing densities as the urban population grows.

Population growth, climatic stress, and weak land administration are likely key drivers of changes in agricultural land use. In the MENA region, population growth and rising incomes tend to increase the demand for agricultural land (for domestic food production) both domestically as well as abroad through imports and foreign direct investment (FDI). Meanwhile, severe climatic factors (land degradation stemming from high temperatures, low precipitation, salinization, and rising sea levels) constrain the feasibility of land cultivation in the MENA region. A background paper prepared for this study (Park et al., forthcoming) mobilizes the MODIS data set globally to study how these factors affect the spatial dynamics of cropland, focusing on gross cropland losses. Although moderate movements in and out of cropland are to be expected with agricultural activities, the study confirms that drought, poor land suitability, salinity (as measured by proximity to coast), and the lack of potential for surface water irrigation (as measured by distance to river) all contribute to land degradation. In addition to these biophysical factors, the study finds that richer and more unequal societies—countries where the demographic pressure on land use is stronger (as inversely measured by the amount of cropland per capita) and countries with poor land administrations—degrade land at a higher pace (see box 1.2 and annex 1B for the methodology and regression results). The impact of land scarcity and poor land governance on cropland loss is illustrated in figure 1.8, which plots a country-level indicator of land degradation on cropland per capita (panel a) and on the Quality of Land Administration indicator (panel b) measured by the World Bank's Doing Business project.[7]

Box 1.2 **The drivers of global cropland loss**

Using the longitudinal information in the MODIS product (see box 1.1), land use transitions into and out of cropland were constructed at the pixel level (500 × 500 meters) for the world between 2003 and 2018. These pixel transitions were then merged with various georeferenced databases that provide measures of local factors potentially driving cropland dynamics. These drivers include *local biophysical variables* (temperature, precipitation, severity of drought, distance to river, distance to coast) and *local demographic and infrastructure characteristics* (travel time to nearest city). The empirical analysis is then performed in two stages, which makes it possible to distinguish between local drivers and country–level drivers.

(box continues on next page)

Box 1.2 The drivers of global cropland loss *(continued)*

Local drivers

Land use transitions (for the world at a 500-meter resolution) are first regressed on all the potential local determinants of land use change in the database and on country fixed effects. These fixed effects—which are used in the second stage of the analysis—capture all national-level determinants that are common to all pixels within the same country. Results from this first stage (table 1B.1 in annex 1B) unambiguously show that cropland loss is strongly correlated with adverse climatic shocks, distance to river (due to aridity and difficulty of irrigation), proximity to coast (due to salinization), and travel time to local markets (due to transport costs).

Country-level drivers

In the second stage, the country fixed effects are recovered from the first stage and regressed on national variables measuring *economic and institutional contexts* (see table 1B.2 in annex 1B). The analysis finds that cropland loss is positively correlated with factors that can induce land degradation through a more intense utilization of land—that is, a low amount of cropland per capita and high GDP per capita. It also finds that unequal societies (high Gini index) tend to degrade land faster, which could suggest that the poor are adopting unsustainable livelihood strategies for land use. Finally, the regression finds that the Doing Business score for the Quality of Land Administration indicator[a] curbs the rate of land degradation, highlighting that functional land administrations play a role in preserving natural resources.

More details can be found in Park et al. (forthcoming).

a. World Bank, Doing Business 2004–2020 (database), https://archive.doingbusiness.org/en/doingbusiness.

Figure 1.8 The effects of land scarcity and land governance on cropland loss, by region

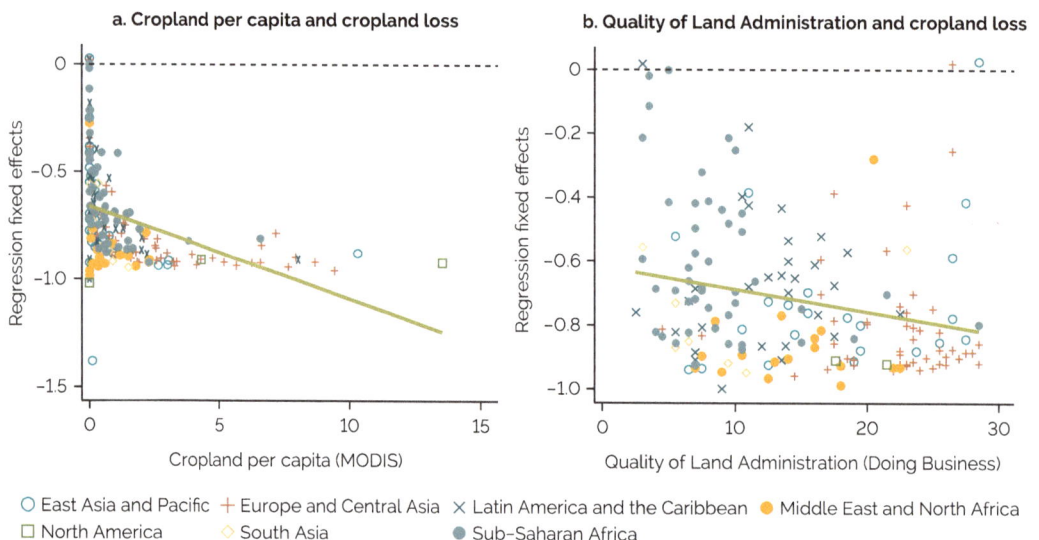

a. Cropland per capita and cropland loss

b. Quality of Land Administration and cropland loss

○ East Asia and Pacific + Europe and Central Asia × Latin America and the Caribbean ● Middle East and North Africa
□ North America ◇ South Asia ● Sub-Saharan Africa

Sources: Panel a: authors' calculations from MODIS Land Cover Type (MCD12Q1) version 6, https://lpdaac.usgs.gov/products /mcd12q1v006/; panel b: authors' calculations from World Bank, Doing Business 2004–2020 (database), https://archive.doingbusiness .org/en/doingbusiness.

Conflicts, which plague the MENA region,[8] affect land use through the loss of property rights and population displacement. They have led to temporary abandonment of cropland in Syria and expansion of cultivated land on the other side of the Syria-Turkey border. Violent events can have large impacts on the use of land, especially in rural areas where land rights can be lost, agricultural productivity can be disrupted, and populations can be forcibly displaced. For example, a recent study found a significant decline in cultivated areas following Saddam Hussein's military assaults on the Kurds in the Kurdistan region of Iraq in 1988 (Eklund, Persson, and Pilesjö 2016). These changes in land use are profound in many cases, with only a small percentage of the abandoned fields being recultivated immediately after the cessation of hostilities.[9]

For this study, Ozden et al. (forthcoming) assessed how the Syrian civil war has affected land use.[10] Their research sought to identify the effects of the conflict on the amount of cultivated land, which is directly measured from space using the MODIS data product. It looked at the location of many of the changes—around the Syria-Turkey border—where it is possible to causally estimate the effect of the conflict on cropland dynamics by comparing areas with similar agroecological conditions on each side of the border (see box 1.3 for a brief description of the methodology). Turkey, however, was likely only indirectly affected by the conflict because large population movements into Turkey and refugee camps located on the Turkish side of the border could have increased the labor supply of the agriculture sector. Map 1.1, which shows cropland transitions in the study area between 2009 (before the conflict) and 2017, confirms that cropland was abandoned (red dots) mostly in Syria, whereas new cropland (black dots) mostly appeared in Turkey, north of the border.

According to Ozden et al. (forthcoming), the conflict in Syria led to a 7 percent decrease in cropland area on the Syrian side and a 5 percent increase in cropland area on the Turkish side, implying a 12 percent gap between the two countries. The effect, however, seems to have been temporary and to have ceased by 2019 (see figure B1.3.1 in box 1.3). In view of the previous literature on conflict and land use, this is surprising and seems to indicate unexpected resilience, possibly under the stabilization efforts of the involved parties.

Box 1.3 The impact of the Syrian conflict on cultivated land

Estimating the impact of a conflict on agricultural land use is challenging because it requires isolating the effect of the conflict from other potential drivers of land use change. To overcome such problems, a geographic regression discontinuity (GRD) design is implemented to compare land use changes in cropland areas (as measured from space by the MODIS data product) on both sides of the Syrian Arab Republic–Turkey border. Because land use data are available annually for each 500 × 500 meter pixel, the GRD design can be combined with a difference-in-differences (DID) approach. This unified empirical framework allows estimation of how the conflict reduces cropland in Syria relative to Turkey every year and to decompose the gap in terms of losses in Syria and gains in Turkey accounting for both violent events in Syria and displacement of population from Syria to Turkey.

Figure B1.3.1 shows the coefficients of interest in the regression. They measure the cumulative percentage change in cropland in Syria (compared with Turkey) arising from the conflict. The graph clearly shows that the cropland dynamics between the two countries began to diverge in 2011 when conflict erupted in Syria, culminating in 2017 with a 12 percent cumulated decrease in cropland area on the Syrian side of the border relative to the Turkish side. A reduction of the effect in 2018 (and even reversal in 2019) suggests that the impact could have been transitory.[a]

(box continues on next page)

Figure B1.3.1 Reduction in cropland in the Syrian Arab Republic relative to Türkiye arising from the Syrian conflict, 2010–19

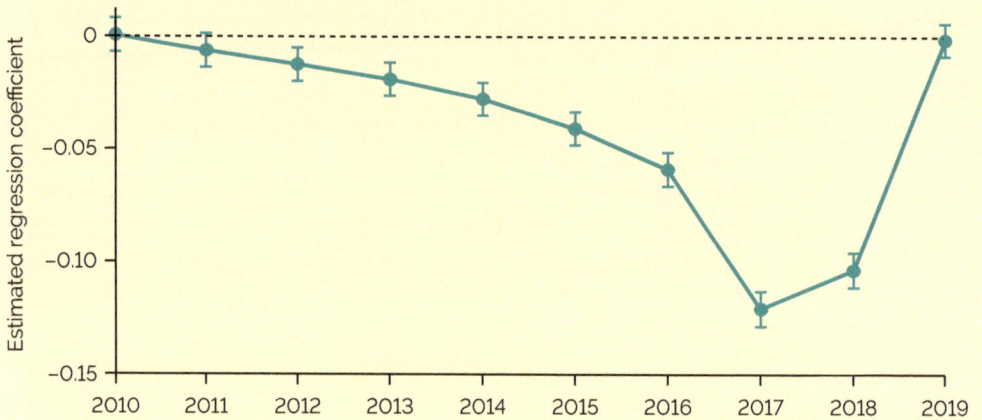

Source: Authors' calculations, based on MODIS Land Cover Type (MCD12Q1) version 6, https://lpdaac.usgs.gov/products /mcd12q1v006/.

Note: The graph shows the estimated coefficient in the combined GRD/DID approach in Ozden et al. (forthcoming). It measures the estimated cumulated percentage reduction in cropland in Syria relative to Turkey resulting from the Syrian conflict. DID = difference-in-differences; GRD = geographic regression discontinuity.

a. See Ozden et al. (forthcoming) for more details.

Map 1.1 Land cover change on each side of the Syrian Arab Republic-Türkiye border, 2009–17

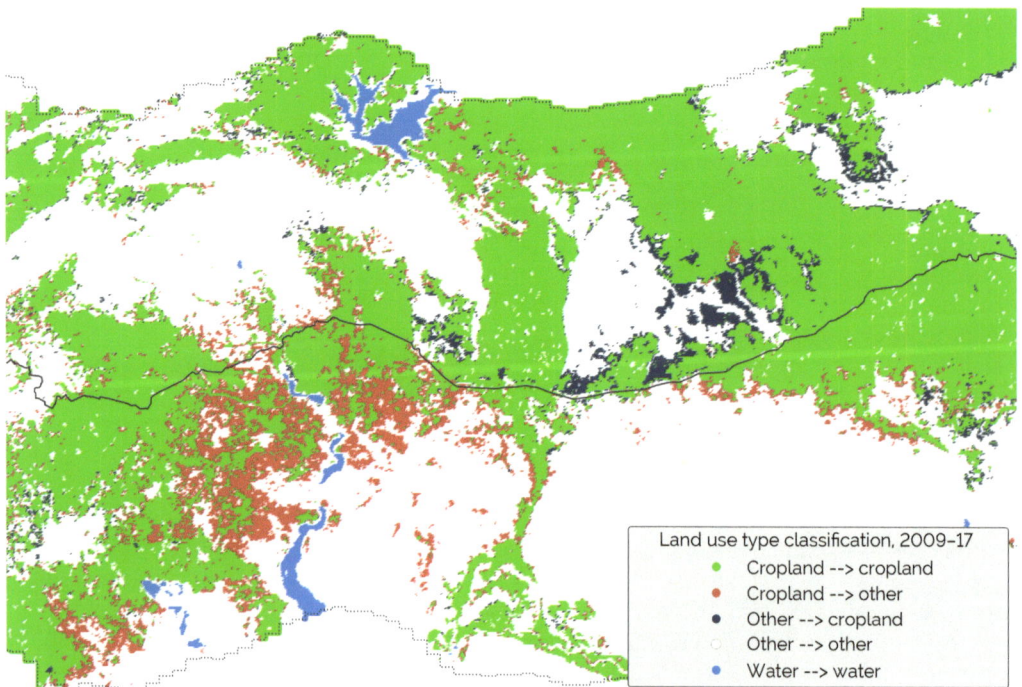

Land use type classification, 2009–17

- Cropland --> cropland
- Cropland --> other
- Other --> cropland
- Other --> other
- Water --> water

Source: MODIS Land Cover Type (MCD12Q1) version 6, https://lpdaac.usgs.gov/products/mcd12q1v006/.

Note: The black line represents the Syria-Turkey border, with Syria to the south and Turkey to the north of the border.

FUTURE TRENDS AND IMPACTS ON THE DEMAND FOR LAND

Land degradation and desertification,[11] long under way in the MENA region, especially in Algeria, Egypt, the Islamic Republic of Iran, Jordan, Morocco, and Syria (IPCC 2019), have high economic costs. These processes stem from both climatic and anthropological factors. Experts predict that volatile temperature fluctuations and drought will continue to cause land degradation, posing major problems to agriculture. In Saudi Arabia, for example, it is estimated that temperatures will rise by 1.8–4.1 degrees Celsius by 2050, leading to an increase of 5–15 percent in the demand for agricultural water, especially affecting oases (IPCC 2019). As for the role of human interventions in land degradation in the MENA region, they include unsustainable agricultural practices (Abu Hammad and Tumeizi 2012; Jendoubi et al. 2020), government policies (Nielsen and Adriansen 2005), and institutions (as the analysis in the previous section confirmed). Land degradation on this scale has a significant economic cost. For example, Réquier-Desjardins and Bied-Charreton (2006) estimate the cost of degradation at about 1 percent of the GDP of Algeria and Egypt and 0.5 percent of the GDP of Morocco and Tunisia. Land degradation costs on average 1 percent of GDP in MENA countries (World Bank 2019).

Because most of the MENA region's cities and agriculture are located along its coasts, coastal recession and the rise in sea level pose a threat to the whole region, increasing the risk of floods, seawater intrusion in aquifers, and the salinization of land. A database of the impacts of a rise in sea level allows predictions of land masses in the region affected by such rises in different scenarios, ranging from a 1-meter to a 5-meter rise.[12] The figures show that between 0.4 and 0.8 percent of the land in the MENA region would be affected. But for some countries, these figures are much more dramatic. For example, Qatar would see between 2.7 and 13.3 percent of its land mass affected. The impacts of a rise in sea level on urban land masses are also significant: a 5-meter rise would affect 13.3 percent of urban land masses in the United Arab Emirates, 11.6 percent in Egypt, and 10.9 percent in Libya. As a result, land availability is being increasingly constrained by the advance of both desert and sea.

Demographic and economic predictions in the MENA region point to a substantial increase in the demand for land in the future. The predicted 40 percent increase in population in the region by 2050 (to 650 million people), coupled with rising incomes (implying more caloric food diets), will certainly increase the demand for land for food production unless the additional demand for food is fully absorbed by imports or an (unlikely) increase in productivity.[13] The increase in urban population in the region is predicted to occur at an even faster pace, rising by more than 60 percent (an increase of 190 million people) by 2050, while the rural population is expected to stagnate or decline. The enormity of the predicted increase in urban population (which is more than the combined current population of France, Spain, and the United Kingdom) implies that under the current urban expansion conditions (see figure 1.7) and the corresponding elasticity of land growth to population growth, the urban footprint in the MENA region will have to expand by more than 50 percent by 2050.[14] Based on the current total built-up area in the region (as measured from space by the MODIS data product), this would correspond to an additional 2.6 million hectares of new urban land.

If climatic and population trends continue as predicted, agricultural land will become significantly scarcer in the MENA region, falling to a level that could lead to a major crisis if not addressed. This looming crisis is illustrated by the dramatic decrease in agricultural land per capita that the region has been experiencing for decades. Figure 1.9 shows the past and projected (until 2050) downward trajectory for agricultural land per capita, taking into

Figure 1.9 Availability of agricultural land per capita, MENA, 1961–2050

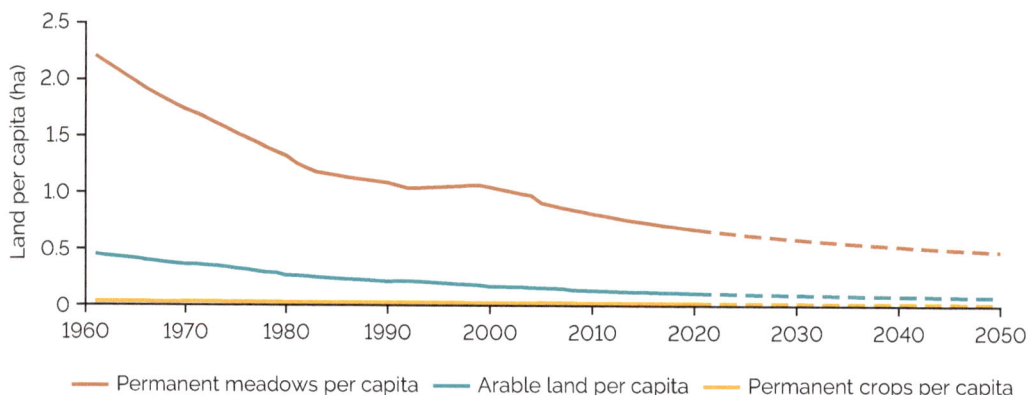

Sources: Authors' calculations, based on Food and Agriculture Organization, FAOSTAT (dashboard), http://www.fao.org/faostat/; United Nations (2019).
Note: ha = hectares.

account projected population growth in the region.[15] This context of increasing scarcity raises important strategic issues about the best use of land to serve economic, social, sustainability, and sovereignty objectives. In concrete terms, the region is faced with the dilemma of how to best use land for housing, industry, commercial activities, or agricultural production while preserving water and pursuing food self-sufficiency and food security goals.[16] The pursuit of food self-sufficiency, in particular, has been a central objective in the MENA region since the 1970s, with significant implications for land use. As discussed in chapter 5, policy responses have taken different forms, from the preservation of agricultural land in peri-urban areas to land reclamation and "export" of land needs through imports of food or direct acquisition of agricultural land abroad.

ANNEX 1A: THE POTENTIAL FOR CROPLAND EXPANSION

Land cover information from the MODIS data product was overlaid with information on land suitability for cultivation from GAEZ V4.0 for an umbrella crop consisting of the 27 main crops in the MENA region cited in OECD/FAO (2018).[17] It revealed that only an additional 6.3 million hectares of MENA grassland are suitable for rainfed agriculture under a high-input cultivation scenario. This figure represents a potential maximum increase of only 16.5 percent of the current cropland area as measured in the MODIS data. Replicating this calculation with seven major international crops leads to only 3.7 million hectares of MENA grassland suitable for rainfed agriculture under a high-input cultivation scenario for these crops, or a potential maximum increase of 9.6 percent of current cropland. Table 1A.1 reports these "expansion margins" by region for these seven major international crops.

Table 1A.1 Land under cultivation and potential for expansion (seven major international crops), by region

Region	Cropland (ha, millions)	Available land for rainfed agriculture (ha, millions)	Ratio to existing cropland (%)
East Asia and Pacific	252.5	237.5	94.1
Europe and Central Asia	365.7	223.1	61.0
Latin America and the Caribbean	106.9	499.6	467.4
Middle East and North Africa	38.3	3.7	9.6
North America	200.1	259.4	129.6
South Asia	235.9	28.5	12.1
Sub-Saharan Africa	131.9	755.8	573.0
World total	**1,331.3**	**2,007.6**	**150.8**

Sources: MODIS Land Cover Type (MCD12Q1) version 6, https://lpdaac.usgs.gov/products/mcd12q1v006/; Food and Agriculture Organization, FAO Global Agro-Ecological Zones (GAEZ) V4.0, https://gaez.fao.org/; International Union for Conservation of Nature (IUCN).
Note: Cropland includes the MODIS categories cropland and cropland mosaic (see box 1.1 for definitions). Available land for rainfed agriculture includes all land classified as grassland in MODIS (outside of protected areas) with good, high, or very high suitability under rainfed agriculture and a high input scenario for at least one of seven major crops, according to GAEZ V4.0. The seven crops are cassava, maize, oil palm, sorghum, soybean, sugarcane, and wheat. ha = hectares.

ANNEX 1B: THE DETERMINANTS OF GLOBAL LAND DEGRADATION

Table 1B.1 Determinants of global land degradation (stage 1)

Dependent variable: Movement out of cropland	
(Intercept)	9.886e-01*** (1.648e-01)
Distance to city	1.497e-07*** (9.628e-10)
Number of drought months	5.473e-04*** (2.151e-06)
Land suitability for agricultural use	−1.499e-03*** (2.584e-06)
Distance to coast	−1.429e-08*** (1.413e-10)
Distance to river	−3.348e-08*** (7.763e-10)
Country fixed effect	Y
No. of observations	48,374,216
R^2	0.06

Sources: Climate Hazards Center, University of California, Santa Barbara, Climate Hazards Group InfraRed Precipitation with Station Data (CHIRPS), https://www.chc.ucsb.edu/data/chirps; Climatology Lab, TERRACLIMATE (dashboard), Palmer Drought Severity Index (PDSI), https://www.climatologylab.org/terraclimate.html; Natural Earth; Food and Agriculture Organization, FAO Global Agro-Ecological Zones (GAEZ) V4.0, https://gaez.fao.org/; Blankespoor, Khan, and Selod (2017).
Note: Standard errors are in parentheses.
***$p < 0.01$.

Table 1B.2 Determinants of global land degradation (stage 2)

Variable	(1)	(2)	(3)	(4)
Cropland per capita	−0.0430*** (0.00726)	−0.0387*** (0.00731)	−0.0375*** (0.00729)	−0.0301*** (0.00684)
Quality of Land Administration		−0.00387* (0.00221)	−0.00727*** (0.00272)	−0.00577** (0.00266)
GDP per capita (current US$)			2.34e-06** (1.07e-06)	1.29e-06 (1.03e-06)
Gini index				0.00386* (0.00222)
Constant	−0.660*** (0.0186)	−0.609*** (0.0354)	−0.590*** (0.0370)	−0.770*** (0.104)
No. of observations	187	171	167	148
R^2	0.160	0.188	0.213	0.237

Sources: Cropland per capita: MODIS 2018 (MODIS Land Cover Type [MCD12Q1] version 6, https://lpdaac.usgs.gov/products /mcd12q1v006/); Quality of Land Administration: World Bank, Doing Business 2004–2020 (database), https://archive.doingbusiness .org/en/doingbusiness; GDP per capita: World Bank, World Development Indicators (database), https://databank.worldbank.org /source/world-development-indicators; Gini index: latest values reported in World Bank, World Development Indicators (database), https://databank.worldbank.org/source/world-development-indicators.
Note: Standard errors are in parentheses.
$*p < 0.1; **p < 0.05; ***p < 0.01$.

NOTES

1. This report adopts the World Bank regional definition for the Middle East and North Africa, which is composed of the following economies: Algeria, Bahrain, Djibouti, the Arab Republic of Egypt, the Islamic Republic of Iran, Iraq, Israel, Jordan, Kuwait, Lebanon, Libya, Malta, Morocco, Oman, Qatar, Saudi Arabia, the Syrian Arab Republic, Tunisia, the United Arab Emirates, the West Bank and Gaza, and the Republic of Yemen.

2. Consistent with this figure, a global data set of urban footprints indicates that the total built-up area of MENA cities grew by 19 percent between 1990 and 2010 (Blankespoor, Khan, and Selod 2017).

3. The phenomenon is the most acute in Egypt, where cities and agriculture coexist in close proximity within the Nile Delta and on the banks of the Nile River.

4. The influence of policies on land use is discussed in subsequent chapters.

5. This is greater than the global annual rate of increase in urban population of 2.1 percent over the period 2000–2020 (United Nations 2019).

6. Contrary to the UN-Habitat analysis, which uses longitudinal data, these elasticities were obtained with cross-sectional data for 2010 using the data set created by Blankespoor, Khan, and Selod (2017). The coefficient greater than 1 for large cities implies an increase in the sprawl of larger cities in the MENA region alongside their population growth.

7. World Bank, Doing Business 2004–2020 (database), https://archive.doingbusiness.org/en/doingbusiness. The indicator of land degradation is the fixed effect from the first-stage regression described in box 1.2. The greater its value, the faster is the cropland loss.

8. Armed conflicts have been plaguing the region for years, especially in Iraq, Libya, Syria, and the Republic of Yemen, which together host 21 percent of the region's population. These conflicts have led to massive population displacements within and from MENA countries: 15 million internally displaced persons (IDPs) and 7.2 million refugees (that is, 37 percent of IDPs and 30 percent of refugees globally).

9. On the other hand, conflict may alternatively lead belligerents to increase agricultural production for purposes of strategic food sufficiency or to use agricultural production as an income source. For example, Jaafar and Woertz (2016) argue that wheat, barley, and cotton production was a crucial income source for the Islamic State of Iraq and the Levant (ISIS) in Syria and Iraq around the period 2014–16. Because of cuts in their food supply, civilians may also react to conflict by expanding self-production, possibly putting new land into cultivation.

10. This case study has potential validity for other countries in the region that undergo comparable hardship. It focuses on cropland abandonment, but there is also evidence that buildings in cities were widely damaged. For example, Lubin and Saleem (2019) found that 45–57 percent of Aleppo was damaged between 2011 and 2017.

11. *Desertification* is defined as land degradation occurring in dryland regions.

12. See S. Dasgupta, B. Laplante, C. Meisner, D. Wheeler, and J. Yan, Sea-Level-Rise (SLR) data set, 2006, https://datacatalog.worldbank.org (WLD_2006_SLR_v01_M); Dasgupta et al. (2009).

13. The average productivity of land in the MENA region is very low, and only greater than that of Sub-Saharan Africa. The Food and Agriculture Organization and Organisation for Economic Co-operation and Development (OECD) report that the annual value of gross production per hectare of agricultural land in the MENA region is about 40 percent that of North America and 10 percent that of Western Europe with its intensive agriculture (OECD/FAO 2018). The MENA region's low productivity reflects land degradation and the choice of low-yield temperate crops, except, for example, the irrigated cereal production in Egypt.

14. This regional estimate is confirmed by city-specific studies—for example, Khawaldah (2016) predicts that Amman's footprint will expand by 44 percent between 2014 and 2030. Such estimates, however, could be further refined, taking into account all the factors underlying urban land demand and density, including predictions of household size, income (land being a normal good whose consumption rises with income), and patterns of human settlement and tenure (formal versus informal settlements, dwelling types, and vertical growth).

15. Figure 1.9 is based on the conservative assumption that arable land, cropland, and meadows will remain constant in the future. The per capita decrease may, however, turn out to be even more pronounced because agricultural land is likely to continue to decrease rather than stay constant.

16. An illustration of this type of dilemma appears in Radwan et al. (2019).

17. MODIS Land Cover Type (MCD12Q1) version 6, https://lpdaac.usgs.gov/products/mcd12q1v006/; Food and Agriculture Organization, FAO Global Agro-Ecological Zones (GAEZ) V4.0, https://gaez.fao.org. Also see Fischer et al. (2021).

REFERENCES

Abu Hammad, A., and A. Tumeizi. 2012. "Land Degradation: Socioeconomic and Environmental Causes and Consequences in the Eastern Mediterranean." *Land Degradation and Development* 23 (3): 216–26.

Blankespoor, B., A. Khan, and H. Selod. 2017. "A Consolidated Dataset of Global Urban Populations: 1969–2015." Technical note, World Bank, Washington, DC.

Dasgupta, S., B. Laplante, C. Meisner, D. Wheeler, and J. Yan. 2009. "The Impact of Sea-Level Rise on Developing Countries: A Comparative Analysis." *Climatic Change* 93 (3): 379–88.

Eklund, L., A. Persson, and P. Pilesjö. 2016. "Cropland Changes in Times of Conflict, Reconstruction, and Economic Development in Iraqi Kurdistan." *Ambio* 45 (1): 78–88.

Fischer, G., F. O. Nachtergaele, H. T. van Velthuizen, F. Chiozza, G. Franceschini, M. Henry, D. Muchoney, and S. Tramberend. 2021. "Global Agro-Ecological Zones v4—Model Documentation." Food and Agriculture Organization, Rome. https://doi.org/10.4060/cb4744en.

IPCC (Intergovernmental Panel on Climate Change). 2019. *Climate Change and Land: An IPCC Special Report on Climate Change, Desertification, Land Degradation, Sustainable Land Management, Food Security, and Greenhouse Gas Fluxes in Terrestrial Ecosystems*, edited by P. R. Shukla et al. Geneva: IPCC.

Jaafar, H. H., and E. Woertz. 2016. "Agriculture as a Funding Source of ISIS: A GIS and Remote Sensing Analysis." *Food Policy* 64: 14–25.

Jendoubi, D., M. S. Hossain, M. Giger, J. Tomićević-Dubljević, M. Ouessar, H. Liniger, and C. I. Speranza. 2020. "Local Livelihoods and Land Users' Perceptions of Land Degradation in Northwest Tunisia." *Environmental Development* 33: 100507.

Khawaldah, H. A. 2016. "A Prediction of Future Land Use/Land Cover in Amman Area Using GIS-Based Markov Model and Remote Sensing." *Journal of Geographic Information System* 8 (3): 412–27.

Lubin, A., and A. Saleem. 2019. "Remote Sensing-Based Mapping of the Destruction to Aleppo during the Syrian Civil War between 2011 and 2017." *Applied Geography* 108: 30–38.

Nielsen, T. T., and H. K. Adriansen. 2005. "Government Policies and Land Degradation in the Middle East." *Land Degradation and Development* 16 (2): 151–61.

OECD (Organisation for Economic Co-operation and Development)/FAO (Food and Agriculture Organization). 2018. *OECD-FAO Agricultural Outlook 2018–2027*. Paris: OECD Publishing; Rome: FAO.

Ozden, C., J. Parada, H. Park, H. Selod, and S. Soumahoro. Forthcoming. "'Scorched and Revived': How the Syrian Conflict Caused Cropland Displacement." Background paper prepared for this report, World Bank, Washington, DC.

Park, H., H. Selod, S. Murray, and G. Chellaraj. Forthcoming. "The Drivers of Land Use Dynamics." Background paper prepared for this report, World Bank, Washington, DC.

Radwan, T. M., G. A. Blackburn, J. D. Whyatt, and P. M. Atkinson. 2019. "Dramatic Loss of Agricultural Land due to Urban Expansion Threatens Food Security in the Nile Delta, Egypt." *Remote Sensing* 11 (3): 332.

Réquier-Desjardins, M., and M. Bied-Charreton. 2006. "Évaluation économique des coûts économiques et sociaux de la désertification en Afrique." Centre d'Economie et d'Ethique pour l'Environnement et le Développement, Université de Versailles St Quentin-en-Yvelines, Paris.

Sulla-Menashe, D., and M. A. Friedl. 2018. *User Guide to Collection 6 MODIS Land Cover (MCD12Q1 and MCD12C1) Product*. Reston, VA: US Geological Survey.

UN-Habitat. 2018. "Metadata on SDGs Indicator 11.3.1 Indicator Category: Tier II." https://unhabitat.org/sites/default/files/2020/07/metadata_on_sdg_indicator_11.3.1.pdf.

United Nations. 2019. *World Urbanization Prospects: The 2018 Revision (ST/ESA/SER.A/420)*. Department of Economic and Social Affairs, Population Division. New York: United Nations.

World Bank. 2019. *Sustainable Land Management and Restoration in the Middle East and North Africa Region: Issues, Challenges, and Recommendations*. Washington, DC: World Bank.

World Bank. 2020. *Convergence: Five Critical Steps toward Integrating Lagging and Leading Areas in the Middle East and North Africa*. Washington, DC: World Bank.

CHAPTER 2

Legal, Institutional, and Governance Challenges Facing Land Use in MENA Countries

INTRODUCTION

This chapter describes the current institutional and legal contexts in the Middle East and North Africa (MENA) governing land issues, highlighting how they have taken shape historically. It also presents the key land governance and land administration challenges in the region.

HISTORICAL FOUNDATIONS OF LEGAL FRAMEWORKS IN THE MENA REGION

The current land tenure systems in MENA countries have been strongly shaped by the region's history and the various regimes that have ruled over time. A review of these historical processes will shed light on the complexity of today's land tenure systems and legal frameworks in MENA countries.

Land tenure regimes in the region are indeed diverse, with many of the political and economic shifts throughout history playing a crucial role in their development.[1] The many empires, kingdoms, caliphates, and states that have ruled the region's territory and people often sought to leverage land to increase agricultural productivity and to raise taxes, both of which were essential for revenue generation. Each polity often brought new methods of land governance that either built on or attempted to replace existing land tenure systems.

This process, however, was never homogeneous for the entire region. Instead, a web of land tenure systems developed that incorporated customary, religious, and state forms of land governance (Sait and Lim 2006). The legal frameworks in today's MENA countries reflect this cumulated history that affected tenure systems in terms of principles, legislation, and practices. In large swaths of the MENA region, Islamic principles codified under the Ottoman Land Code (1858) and customary practices have influenced how land systems and land relations have evolved throughout the region's history and are still important elements of current laws and practices (Waldner 2004).

As noted, governments throughout the MENA region have long encouraged the productive use of land for agriculture to generate revenue through taxation. Since at least the time of the Sasanian Empire prior to the seventh century CE, governments have promoted land reclamation, repurposing unused (*mawat*) land (so-called dead land) for agriculture and allowing private land ownership for those who would reclaim land (Adamo and Al-Ansari 2020). Typically, these landholders would be subject to lower tax rates. Over time, however, small landowners were increasingly strained by higher taxes that exceeded their income, forcing them to sell their land to larger landowners, who had the financial capacity to pay the taxes. As a result, large land estates sprang up throughout the MENA region. These estates were, in turn, perceived to be a threat to the legitimacy of the local ruling authorities, who, in response, undertook further land reforms to abate the growing influence of the large land estates and encourage again smallholdings of land. This cycle of concentration of large landholdings followed by fragmentation and subsequent reforms played out in the MENA region until the postindependence era.

Although private property has been recognized in the MENA region for centuries, it has coexisted with collective forms of tenure supported under *shari'a* and under customary regimes. Collective forms of tenure rather than private ownership nevertheless remained predominant until the mid- to late twentieth century, particularly in rural areas. With the rise of the Islamic caliphates in the mid-seventh century CE, *shari'a* law did not replace the customary land principles and systems, but instead recognized them throughout the region, so long as they did not contradict Islamic principles (Salisu 2013). Thus many land tenure arrangements for tribal and familial communities remained largely the same and maintained the same degree of legitimacy as before the advent of Islam. These customary forms of tenure (*'urf*) often provided specifications for how land could be used (for cultivation, grazing, and so forth) and who could use it. In general, these tenure arrangements were confined to specific communities and were meant and served to avoid the loss of land to external actors.

The last two centuries have seen more emphasis on privatization (over collective forms of tenure) and property registration, which began during the Ottoman Empire, particularly after enactment of the Ottoman Land Code of 1858. As the Ottoman Empire sought to modernize its economy and encourage foreign direct investment from Europe, it also sought through its Land Code to promote individual ownership by denoting a single owner during property registration (*tapu*) with the purpose of encouraging land and real estate market development. Although the reform benefited real estate markets in cities, its results were more nuanced in rural areas of the Empire, with either many tribal leaders registering vast swaths of land in their own names or many communities ignoring the legitimacy of the Land Code entirely. Nevertheless, attempts at the individualization of land ownership under the Ottoman Land Code would lay the foundation for the colonial era during the first half of the twentieth century.

Five broad land tenure categories codified under Ottoman rule are still in use in the MENA region. These categories, which originated in *shari'a* law, are (1) *mulk*, privately owned land held in absolute ownership; (2) *waqf*, religiously endowed land held in charitable trust; (3) *miri*, state-owned land that carries *tasarruf*, which is the right of the landholder to use, exploit, and dispose of the land (*usufruct*); (4) *matruka,* common land; and (5) *mawat*, "dead" and unclaimed land. Box 2.1 provides more details about each land category.

Box 2.1 Land tenure categories under the Ottoman Land Code of 1858

Despite its many innovations to modernize the Ottoman Empire's legal framework for the land sector, the Ottoman Land Code of 1858 was designed to maintain consistency with *shari'a*, from which it was inspired. As part of attempts at consistency, the Land Code maintained *shari'a*'s four land tenure categories, while also adding *mawat* land as a fifth category.

Mulk. This category consists of privately owned land held in absolute ownership. *Mulk* was typically subject to *'ushr*, a religious tax that formed part of the *zakat* (annual religious tax) but specifically applied to land. It was more commonly found in urban areas than in rural areas. However, *mulk* status in rural areas could be achieved through efforts to revive *mawat* land through investment and development for agricultural productivity.

Waqf. This category denotes dedicated land with *usufruct* rights assured to religious or benevolent foundations. In theory, only *mulk* land could be transformed into *waqf* land, but the actual history and distribution of *waqf* land suggest that there was considerable flexibility in practice. The process of converting land into *waqf* involved a "founder" deciding to endow his personal property. The specific purpose for which the land was used and its conditions of management were registered in a deed of endowment submitted to the ruling authorities. The use of all revenues generated from the *waqf* endowment were clearly defined by the founder and could be allocated for a pious purpose or to a group of beneficiaries. The management of *waqf* was entrusted to trustees. Generally, the practice of *waqf* continues to be found throughout the MENA region and may also include properties of other faiths, such as Christian monasteries.

Miri. This category refers to lands collectively owned by the entire Muslim community represented by the state, which held the right to use, exploit, and dispose of the land (*tasarruf*). The *usufructuary* enjoyed the status of quasi-owner, who could sell, rent, mortgage, and issue use rights of the land to others. The *usufructuary*'s rights could be passed down to inheritors, but ownership remained with the caliphate. In addition, the validity of any transfer of *usufruct* rights had to be certified by state authorities or representatives of the state. Historically, most agricultural lands in the MENA region fell in the *miri* category.

Matruka, also called **metruka.** This category included all lands considered common properties of the Muslim community, including most steppe and desert lands. It also included what was considered by the Ottomans to be "abandoned" land designated for the public activities of villages. Specific use rules were applied to *matruka* land in the Ottoman Land Code, including grazing, wood collecting, and designation of public use such as places of worship and public markets.

Mawat. Although considered a land tenure category under *shari'a*, *mawat*, which refers to "dead" or unproductive land, cuts across the other four categories. In the past, *mawat* land was typically converted into *mulk* land if the owner could reclaim the land and make it productive. However, only certain types of productive uses (such as planting trees, plowing the soil, or digging wells) were considered eligible for *mulk* status. Other practices such as demarcating borders with stones or using the land for pasture were not.

Source: Johnson and Ayachi (forthcoming).

Legal provisions designed during the colonial period were used to accommodate land appropriation for settlers and reward local clienteles. Following the dissolution of the Ottoman Empire, attempts were made under French and British colonial rule to clarify land ownership and apply it to colonists who migrated to newly controlled territories. In the French colonies in North Africa, for example, mixed courts were developed to settle disputes between colonists and local communities, although the rulings were often in favor of the colonists (Hursh 2014). Under British mandates, a settlement process was enacted to determine ownership and issue a title deed to properties, further serving the development of land and real estate markets (Sait and Lim 2006). As a result, privatization of land throughout the MENA region ensued, while collective forms of tenure were eroded or attempts were made to dismantle them. The various forms of registration systems introduced by the French and British, however, largely remain intact today and have become the standard for the recognition of formal rights, often in parallel with the customary systems.

During the postindependence period, the state began to increase considerably its control over land and land matters. Carrying over from the colonial era, land reforms to spur agricultural productivity and land and real estate markets continued, but with a scaled-up focus on the privatization of land and the sedentarization of nomadic communities under clear land and property boundaries. Colonial properties were also nationalized, and many tribal lands were incorporated into public land. In addition, to maintain the paramount legitimacy of the legal and institutional frameworks of the state, many governments attempted to incorporate the principles of *shari'a* and customary law through "bureaucratization" (incorporation into state laws). It was particularly applied to the management of *waqf* (and especially limiting or eliminating private *waqf*), land use conversion, land and property transactions, and the appropriation of nonprivate land (*miri, mawat,* and *matruka*). Islamic and customary inheritance principles, although not subject to bureaucratization, remained highly influential, with modern legal frameworks incorporating them into their provisions. In fact, many such provisions remain in effect today.

Sedentarization and bureaucratization efforts are still under way, although with mixed results. One reason for the failure of sedentarization efforts is that they were not accompanied by the provision of technical expertise to ensure productive and income-generating use of the land, and so many settled nomads sold off their land. Examples include land redistribution attempts in Saudi Arabia during the second half of the twentieth century, in which soil aridity and water scarcity made agriculture unviable (Hajrah 1974), and in the Arab Republic of Egypt following the mobilization of land for the government's agriculture and tourism initiatives in the early 1970s and early 1990s (Revkin 2014). Moreover, bureaucratization has led to corruption or dispute in land transactions (Balgley 2015). In Morocco, for example, the government's infrastructure initiatives, in partnership with private sector actors, have occasionally resulted in the Ministry of Habous and Islamic Affairs recategorizing *waqf* land as *mulk*. This tenure change—which was driven by political and economic interests to allow the implementation of development projects—has disrupted land rights and uses under *waqf* arrangements (Balgley 2015).

The postindependence period also saw land reforms that affected the distribution and use of land (through nationalization and redistribution). The reforms were meant to benefit smallholders and farmers and to spur agricultural productivity because agriculture was still the major economic sector in most countries in the region. In the process, however, nearly all MENA countries expropriated land once belonging to foreigners to benefit the public domain. In Algeria, for example, the socialist government took control of farms abandoned by French colonists and turned them into peasant cooperatives. Large land estates were also taken over by the military and nationalized. In Egypt, the government led by Gamal Abdel Nasser also enacted land reforms that expropriated all landholdings larger than 200 feddans (84 hectares) to redistribute them to smallholders. However, these reform attempts did not spur the intended agricultural development objectives. In Algeria, the cooperative system was not deemed sufficient to meet the demands of Algerian farmers because the low levels of agricultural output were not sufficiently viable commercially to be a sustainable form of employment (Benessaiah 2015). It was thus later replaced by a system of individual concessions that for 40 years incentivized farmers to engage in private enterprise so they could profit entirely from their agricultural outputs. In Egypt, the allocation of 2 feddans (0.84 hectares) to farmers was not enough to develop agriculture to scale, and Nasser's reforms soon fell into cronyism and patrimonialism, with large swaths of land distributed to political allies and stakeholders with vested interests.

Land confiscation and reallocation, along with control over natural resources, has also played a core role in the MENA region's most recent wars. Land and property have been particularly important in the patronage systems of governance in Iraq, Libya, the Syrian Arab Republic, and the Republic of Yemen, where authoritarian regimes used land confiscation, occupation, and population replacement to favor supporting groups and control the opposition. For example, in Libya Muammar Gaddafi utilized such techniques in 1969 to expropriate assets from the Italian and Libyan landed elites, and he did the same to opponents in 1978.[2] In 2006, Gaddafi created a compensation committee to address the law's "misapplication." However, this gesture did not lead to any real change or proper compensation. Similarly, in Iraq expropriation of minorities' and opponents' land started with agrarian reforms that were introduced as early as 1958. These policies later morphed into Arabization of the Kurdish areas around Kirkuk in the 1980s.

In summary, a historical review of land systems reveals three key issues the MENA region is still facing today: legal pluralism, the prominence of the state, and the challenges of land taxation. As for the first issue, the existing legal pluralism and coexistence of tenure situations (formal, customary, and religious) have their roots in the superposition of various tenure systems throughout history, which had significant impacts in the Ottoman, colonial, and postindependence periods. Many newly independent states and governments, in their attempts to consolidate their authority and legitimacy, sought to build on the tenure systems introduced by the French and British, while also incorporating *shari'a* and *'urf* because it was important to not be seen as perpetuating a colonial system that had negatively affected much of the local populace.

As for the second issue, a look back at history reveals that states have usually been heavily involved in the land sector, whether through direct ownership of public land or through policies aimed at changing the nature of land rights and the redistribution of land itself. This omnipresence of states in land affairs, along with the involvement of numerous institutions in the land sector, is still a key feature of most MENA countries today.

As for the third issue, throughout history attempts at land reform have sought to generate tax revenue for newly independent MENA states. However, the key economic sectors on which this reform was based, such as agriculture, have since lost their dominance in most MENA countries. As a result, solutions for mitigating losses in revenue, such as policies for property taxation in urban areas, remain largely absent throughout the region.

LAND GOVERNANCE CHALLENGES

Major challenges common to MENA countries weaken land governance, resulting in inefficient and opaque land administration and management. The four main challenges are (1) complex, outdated legal frameworks; (2) institutional fragmentation with overlapping mandates; (3) disproportionate involvement of the state in the land sector; and (4) weakness of property taxation. As just described, these challenges have historical roots and reflect current political economy constraints that prevent or slow down reforms.

Complex, Outdated Legal Frameworks

The complexity of legal frameworks governing land in MENA countries is the result of the accumulation over time of layers of customary and statutory regimes, as well as the ongoing use of fragmented land tenure categories. The accumulation of layers of customary and statutory regimes stems from the nineteenth-century Ottoman laws, the early twentieth-century colonial laws, and the more recent postindependence laws. In Morocco, for example, laws stemming from custom, *shari'a*, the French colonial period, and the postindependence period have created a legal pluralism governing land tenure, land administration, and land management. Because of all these layers, the recognition and registration of land ownership and access—especially for agricultural land and land subject to various customary tenure regimes—are highly complex. The same issue is evident in the West Bank and Gaza, where the legal framework still incorporates provisions from Ottoman, British, Jordanian, Egyptian, and Israeli laws, in addition to Palestinian Authority laws and decrees. The complexity is also compounded by the continued use in many MENA countries of the five land tenure categories of the Ottoman Land Code (see box 2.1), despite their relative disconnect from the modern context. Finally, this complexity is exacerbated by the fact that customary regimes, which are enduring in most MENA countries—just as in many nations throughout Sub-Saharan Africa, Latin America, and Asia—are not always recognized in the law.

A major implication of this complexity in legal frameworks is that it can result in overlaps or gaps in legislation, muddy citizens' understanding of the law, and make its enforcement very difficult. For example, the extent to which Morocco's formal land laws are applied and interpreted depends on location, ownership, and local control over land matters. In the country's rural Middle Atlas region, some village councils may apply customary rules of land access and use that are contrary to official government policy, while in irrigated agricultural areas formal law is more likely to be enforced (USAID 2011).

Another example of gaps in legal frameworks is the status of *musha'* (communal) land in Lebanon. Although it is estimated that *musha'* makes up approximately 20 percent of Lebanon's total land area, its present status as an independent land category in Lebanon's land registry is not clear in the legal framework. Instead, *musha'* is often considered to be state-owned land with varying degrees of control by municipalities. Although various laws have been drafted to help to clarify the status of *musha'*,[3] they have been ad hoc and specific to certain areas of Lebanon, such as the villages of Mount Lebanon. Because no comprehensive legislation is yet available, many communities remain uncertain about *musha'*'s official status. This complexity, coupled with a disincentive for people to undergo cumbersome formal land registration processes, fuels informal tenure, often to people's own detriment and that of the system at large.

The complexity of tenure situations often leads to lack of clarity of property rights and facilitates the emergence of competing claims over property rights and conflicts. For example, in Egypt tensions emerged because of competing claims between traditional rights and unregistered land transactions (Johannsen, Nabil Mahrous, and Graversen 2009). Tensions over competing claims tend to become especially problematic in the wake of regime change, when ownership rights may become even more muddled. For example, in Tunisia the village of Jemna sits on collective land appropriated from local tribes under colonization, then transferred to the state after independence, and finally reclaimed by villagers during the Arab Spring (Foroudi 2020). Similarly, in 1967 the socialist regime of the People's Democratic Republic of Yemen expelled tribal sheikhs and sultans from their lands, abolished sultanates, and converted the property into state land. The sultans moved to Saudi Arabia, but they were invited back in 1990 when the country reunified. Upon their return, many tribal sheikhs and sultans attempted to regain their lands through legal means, but they faced a corrupt justice system that refused to return customary ownership of state lands. As a result, many sought support from Al-Qaeda to solve the conflict, leading to confrontation with the Houthis (Unruh 2016).

In addition to their complexity, existing land-related laws are generally outdated and disconnected from current contexts. They also render the recognition and enforcement of property rights ineffective. Instead of completely overhauling these legal frameworks and reorienting them to adequately meet current challenges, most countries have simply introduced amendments to address issues as they have emerged. For example, Lebanon still relies on legislation dating from the French mandate period, including a real estate registration law enacted in 1926. Because the law was formulated a century ago, it is out of sync with the current context such as digitized land services and e-government. Similarly, across the MENA region laws do not cover practices that have become essential and ubiquitous as a result of economic development, such as urban planning and building codes in Iraq or tenant farming in Lebanon. As a result, the legal frameworks that govern land in most MENA countries are not aligned with reality and the current needs of their respective economies. When existing laws are amended, the changes commonly create confusion because the courts and institutions in charge of implementation may offer different interpretations. These challenges also contribute to making the recognition and enforcement of property rights difficult, if not impossible.

The efforts undertaken throughout the MENA region to modernize outdated legal frameworks and laws related to land and property rights have been slow. The delays stem not only from the substantial amount of time needed to reconcile contradictory laws but also from the political sensitivities of land reforms. A recent example is the ongoing initiative in Egypt that aims to unify the country's coexisting deed and title registration procedures, the complexity of which has nearly pushed the system to obsolescence (see box 2.2). In 2014, a committee representing key agencies involved in land governance was convened to draft a unified land administration bill. Although the bill was prepared, the committee's work was put on hold by the government and the bill was never finalized (Nada and Sims 2020). Similarly, under the "National Land Policy Framework" of the Palestinian National Authority (2008), four draft laws pertaining to major land governance reforms have been drafted but have yet to be adopted.

Box 2.2 The complexities of the Arab Republic of Egypt's deed and title registration systems

Egypt simultaneously operates deed and title registration systems governed by two separate laws (Law No. 114/1946 and Law No. 142/1964, respectively). Both laws bestow responsibilities for registration on the Real Estate Publicity Department (REPD) that sits under the Ministry of Justice. Deed registration is Egypt's most prominent property registration system because it allows the registration of a building or a part thereof (such as an apartment) as a real estate unit. Consequently, Egypt's deed system covers most of the country's urban areas and is also

(box continues on next page)

being introduced for properties in new urban communities and for various development projects in the desert. Under this system, however, deeds are entered chronologically in the order in which they are accepted for registration and indexed according to the names of parties to the deed. This system complicates the task of investigating ownership. Moreover, the deed system in Egypt requires evidence of ownership of the property that is the subject of the transaction, and either the property owner must present a copy of the deed, or registry staff must undertake the cumbersome process of searching through an alphabetical index.

To mitigate the challenges with proof of ownership under the deed system, the government of Egypt is eager to replace it with the title system, which is considered a more authoritative record of ownership and real estate rights. The title system is property-based, and information in the REPD's register is indexed according to a unique parcel or real estate unit identification number. The drawback of the title registration system, however, is that in Egypt it does not permit a building, or a part thereof, to be registered as a real estate unit, thereby discouraging its use in Egypt's urban areas and resulting in its coverage of primarily agricultural land. Thus any attempt to replace the deed system with the title registration system must include a revision of the legal framework to allow the registration of buildings under the title system.

In addition to the complexities of replacing one system with the other, the procedures for registering property under either system are considered highly complex and onerous. Property owners who wish to register or conduct a transaction are required to present a clear chain of title or deed from the last time their property was entered into the registry. However, for all properties in informal areas, particularly in major cities such as Cairo, and even for many formal properties, establishing this chain, which can go back for decades, is simply impossible. Consequently, most land records held at REPD are considered out-of-date and inaccurate. Despite the government piloting of potential resolutions, no major reforms have yet been implemented to address the complexities of navigating the country's property registration systems. As a result, only about 10 percent of all land and properties in Egypt are considered formally registered.

Sources: Nada and Sims (2020); World Bank (2018).

Institutional Fragmentation

Many MENA countries suffer from institutional fragmentation and competition among agencies for control over land, which prevents integrated approaches to land administration and management and leads to poor quality of land administration services. In most countries, multiple, disjointed institutions with independent land mandates operate in an uncoordinated manner. This kind of operation often results in duplication of efforts, cumbersome bureaucratic processes, and even competition between institutions for the management of land. In Iraq, for example, the Ministry of Finance is responsible for recording, protecting, and allocating state land and property. However, several other Iraqi ministries control state land and property for their own purposes and do so through the development of separate land databases that are not linked to the Ministry of Finance because of the perceived risk that they will lose control over their holdings. This lack of coordination between relevant Iraqi institutions makes any inventorying of state land difficult and enables encroachment and violations by contract holders on state land and property.

When there is coordination among ministries and agencies, it is generally ad hoc and inefficient. For example, Egypt's National Center for Planning State Land Uses (NCPSLU) was established in 2001 to act as the coordinating agency for the government's public land development projects. Its board of directors became the main vehicle for discussing proposals by various custodial agencies to acquire and amend their jurisdictions over state lands. Although there has been some improvement in coordination between the different agencies with the establishment of NCPSLU, a lack of coherent coordination persists on public land allocation. The result has been an inefficient pattern of territorial development and little alignment between the objectives and mandates of the custodial agencies that are supposed to coordinate with NCPSLU (Nada and Sims 2020).

This fragmentation, coupled with overlapping—and sometimes contradictory—laws has produced ambiguities about which institution has the mandate over land matters. This confusion prevents the implementation of integrated or holistic approaches to managing land. For example, decisions on urban land development and urban expansion are often made by institutions that do not take into account the impacts of those decisions on agricultural land destruction and food production. Institutional fragmentation, combined with weak rule of law, also explains the lack of transparency in the management of land and provision of land administration services, as discussed in the final section of this chapter.

The lack of coordination across institutions with land mandates is exacerbated by the poor reliability of land administration infrastructure, which does not support information sharing. As described later in this chapter in more detail, digitization of property registration, ownership records and cadasters, spatial plans, and other vital land administration records are not yet complete in several countries in the MENA region.

Role of the State and Centralization of Land Administration and Management

Central state institutions throughout the MENA region enjoy a significant amount of control over land, including valuable land in both urban and rural areas. In fact, state ownership and public use of land are more widespread in the MENA region than in any other region worldwide (see figure 2.1). Although the exact rates of public ownership of land are difficult to determine because of incomplete registration and lack of transparency, public ownership in the MENA region largely stems from historical developments such as the nationalization of colonial properties, the incorporation of tribal lands into public land, and the appropriation of nonprivate lands—including *miri, mevat (mawat),* and *matruka* properties—as well as some *waqf* properties in the postindependence era. As a result, many states own valuable land, such as fertile land for

Figure 2.1 Land under public ownership index, by region

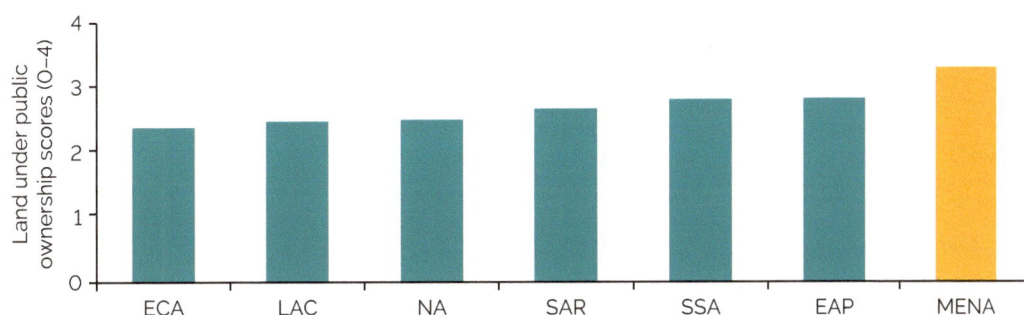

Source: CEPII, Agence Française Développement, and Ministère de l'Économie et des Finances, Institutional Profiles Database (dashboard), http://www.cepii.fr/institutions/en/ipd.asp.
Note: EAP = East Asia and Pacific; ECA = Europe and Central Asia; LAC = Latin America and the Caribbean; MENA = Middle East and North Africa; NA = North America; SAR = South Asia; SSA = Sub-Saharan Africa.

agricultural use, land rich in underground resources, and land situated in prime geographic locations. A large share of valuable properties is believed to be controlled by the military, especially in regimes where the military plays an important political role. For example, as shown in map 2.1, military land occupies a significant portion of the urban space in Algiers.

Public authorities often lack comprehensive records of the land and property they own and the true value of these assets, which affects their ability to make informed decisions about land use and disposal. Despite high levels of state ownership, inventories of state-owned land tend to be either inaccurate or incomplete, and the boundaries are not delineated. Thus because many governments throughout the MENA region do not know what land they own, they cannot leverage public land to provide services or implement social programs. In Iraq, for example, although 80–90 percent of all land is state-owned, no reliable inventory of public land is available.[4] The government is, then, unable to implement social housing programs to resettle Iraqis who have been uprooted by the country's decades-long conflicts. This difficulty, in turn, exacerbates the pervasive encroachments on state land and informal settlements as those desperate for housing take the law into their own hands.

Map 2.1 Land reportedly owned by the military, Algiers, Algeria

Source: OpenStreetMap (crowd-sourced database), 2020, https://www.openstreetmap.org/#map=3/71.34/-96.82.
Note: Areas in yellow and red reportedly belong to the Algerian military.

Overall, governments fail to appropriately supply their economy with land. In several countries, such as Morocco, urban development has long relied on the provision of land by public authorities—land that is often no longer available in suitable locations. When public land is mobilized, the allocation often does not follow market principles—that is, land is not transferred at market value (generating the redistribution of rents and wealth to the beneficiaries of such allocations), or it is not transferred to the most productive users who should be willing to pay more for it. Policy makers often justify the practice of below-market allocation by claiming that they are ensuring the affordability of land for the lower- and middle-income classes and equity of access, although whether these are the actual outcomes is not monitored. An example of below-market allocation is Egypt's switch from a practice of auctions to allocate plots to developers to one of lotteries because auctions were deemed to contribute to price escalation. At the same time, mobilizing private land is extremely difficult in the face of governance challenges (such as lack of clarity of tenure, inefficiency of registration services, and lack of valuation) that inhibit the pooling of land.

Governments have resorted to land allocation to pursue social objectives, but with nuanced results and often through unsustainable mechanisms. For example, in 1986 Oman began to randomly allocate free plots to its citizens using a lottery system. As for other rent economies in the region, this redistribution of wealth has been a means of supporting social stability by fulfilling social expectations. However, this practice may be at an end because the most desirable plots have already been redistributed or handed out to the elite. This practice also came at a high cost to the government because of the pressure exerted by the beneficiaries to have these plots provided with infrastructure. Other inefficient land allocation practices are also driven by the pursuit of food independence objectives, which have resulted in conditional agricultural leases. In Tunisia, for example, lease beneficiaries can be required to engage in types of production for which they may not have a comparative advantage (such as the owner of land suitable for crop cultivation having to partly engage in dairy production).

Central state institutions tend to be the primary authorities in land-related matters, whereas local authorities generally have narrow mandates over land, which undermines development responses tailored to the local environmental and social contexts. For example, in Egypt central institutions control desert land and reclamation processes, as well as desert land within 2 kilometers of agricultural boundaries called *zemam*.[5] In addition, local institutions have no authority to plan land use for activities such as tourism, industry, or new settlements. Instead, they must rely on guidance from central agencies, who may not understand local conditions, but who are nevertheless rarely accountable to local officials and communities (El-Meehy 2013).

Nontransparent control of land by state actors in the context of weak land governance and states' strong grip over land resources contributes to corruption and facilitates elite capture and cronyism. A review of the most recent country reports from the Bertelsmann Transformation Index project[6] reveals that of 17 MENA countries covered, 16 saw corruption, political interference, or cronyism invade property rights. In figure 2.2, for the world, and for MENA countries in particular, a negative correlation emerges between the strength of property rights (as measured by the Bertelsmann Transformation Index, BTI) and perceptions of corruption (as measured by Transparency International's Corruption Perceptions Index).[7] Although this correlation does not imply causality, it suggests that weak land governance is fertile ground for corruption. The opaque processes of land conversion for urban use,

Figure 2.2 Corruption and poor protection of property rights, by all regions and MENA region

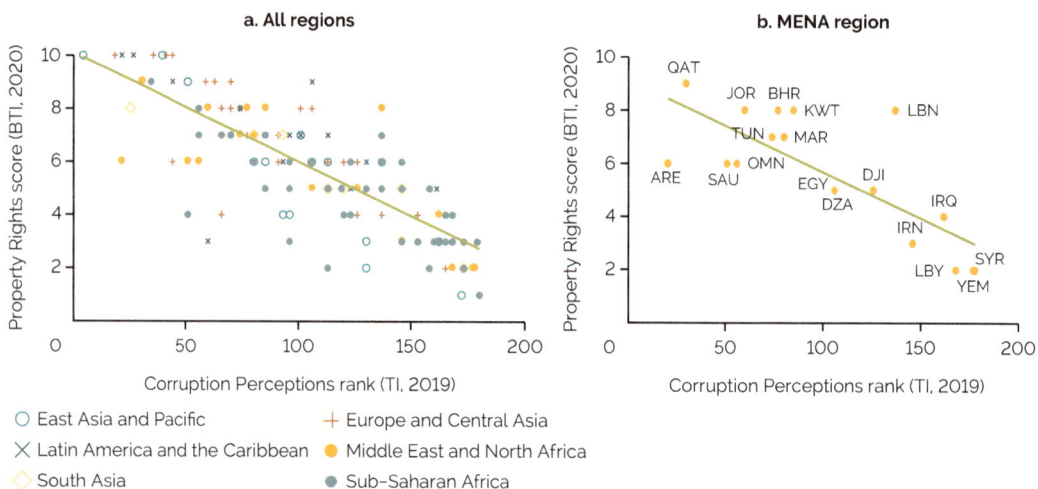

a. All regions

b. MENA region

○ East Asia and Pacific   + Europe and Central Asia
✕ Latin America and the Caribbean   ● Middle East and North Africa
◇ South Asia   ● Sub-Saharan Africa

Sources: Bertelsmann Stiftung, Bertelsmann Transformation Index (BTI) 2020 Country Reports, MENA, http://bti-project.org/; Transparency International (TI), Corruption Perceptions Index (dashboard), 2019, https://www.transparency.org/en/cpi/2019.
Note: These graphs plot BTI's Property Rights score against country rank for TI's Corruption Perceptions Index. The Property Rights score measures the extent to which government authorities ensure well-defined rights of private property and regulate the acquisition, benefits, use, and sale of property. It ranges between 0 (poor) and 10 (excellent). See figure 1.4 for country codes.

in particular, are especially ripe for corruption. Corruption is further aided by discretionary state land allocation practices. For the West Bank and Gaza, for example, the Coalition for Integrity and Accountability, AMAN (2014, 33) finds that the management of state land is imbued with "a conscious policy on behalf of the regime to employ state resources to buy loyalty and reinforce its authority by increasing the number and wealth of influential decision-making loyalists." One way this can be done is by selling state-owned land to strategic individuals at exceedingly low prices, enabling them to turn a massive profit on subsequent sales (Puddephatt 2012).

Weakness of Property Taxation

Property taxation to generate revenue is little used or even absent in MENA countries with some exceptions, such as Israel (figure 2.3). The region lacks a tradition of property taxation, (especially in rent economies in the Gulf Cooperation Council, GCC[8]), and some countries have technical difficulties implementing property taxation because of the low coverage of registries.[9] In the United Arab Emirates, for example, property tax revenue is almost nonexistent and represents only 0.02 percent of the country's GDP, which is extremely low compared with that of other countries such as the United Kingdom, where the revenue from property tax is 4 percent of GDP. After Israel, the country in the region with the most revenue from property taxation is Morocco, at only 1.6 percent of GDP.

Figure 2.3 Property taxation, by region and selected economies, 2020

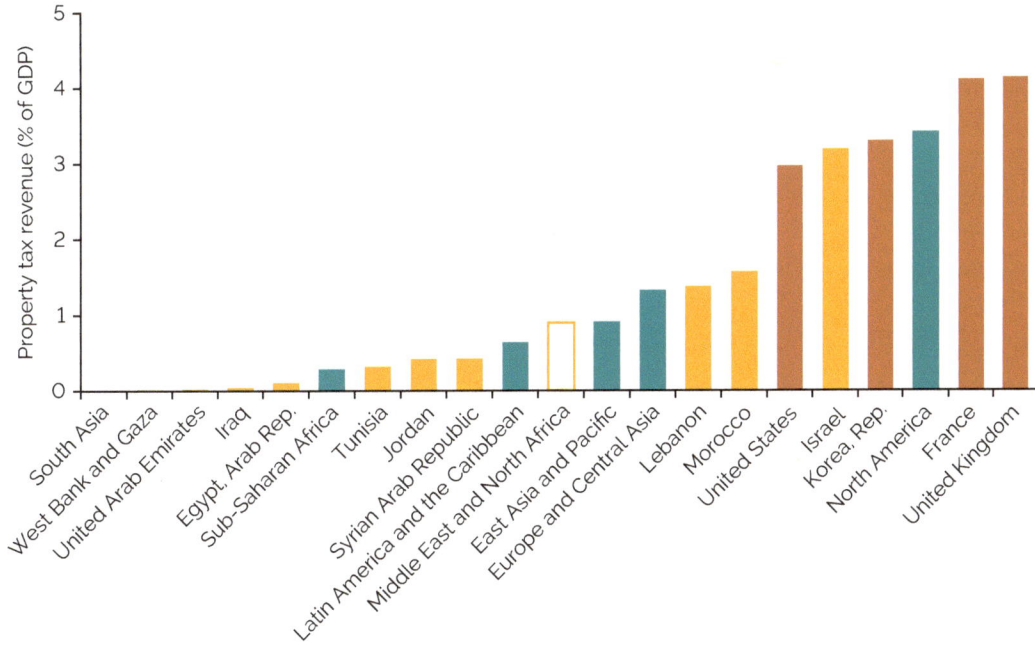

Source: International Monetary Fund, World Revenue Longitudinal Data (WoRLD) (dashboard), 2016–18, https://data.imf.org/?sk =77413F1D-1525-450A-A23A-47AEED40FE78.

These low levels are explained in part by the numerous exemptions introduced to placate vested interests or avoid social discontent, which ultimately defeats the purpose of the tax. Morocco, for example, includes a 75 percent value reduction for primary residences and a five-year exemption for newly constructed property. In Egypt, the real estate tax does not apply to a large majority of housing units (those valued below LE 2 million, or about US$128,000). It also does not apply to many tourism sector properties, such as hotels and resorts, which are considered major generators of revenue for the Egyptian economy, which the legislature does not want to discourage. This system produced very low revenue, US$240 million, in 2018, which is considerably lower than Dubai's revenue of US$4 billion generated each year from real estate taxes. However, all countries in the region except Saudi Arabia have some kind of tax on real estate transactions, which is easier to implement than property taxation and more politically acceptable.

Weak Land Valuation Infrastructure

In general, land valuation in MENA countries is not aligned with international standards, and it is weak in several of them. In many countries, the capacity for valuation is lacking, and the systems are not in place to implement market valuation for taxation purposes. Indeed, governments often base taxation on administrative or outdated book value. The use of underestimated values in property taxation and registration fees introduces distortions in the economy and potentially leads to ineffective land management (including decisions about the disposal and management of state land).

The disconnect between property valuation and market values is even greater when reevaluation periods are far apart (and sometimes do not even follow the legally mandated frequency). In Egypt, for example, although agricultural land is supposed to be reevaluated every 10 years, the last reevaluation only happened in 2014 after a 25-year gap. Some countries do not even have general reevaluation, such as in Lebanon, where properties are valued only when transferred.

The geographic coverage of valuation may also be limited such as in the West Bank, where properties are only valued in half of municipalities and where property values have not been updated in 50 years. These gaps significantly reduce the revenue generated from property taxation.

Most countries suffer from a lack of transparency on market information on land more generally. For example, Lebanon does not produce any market index from real estate transactions. By contrast, in Saudi Arabia land transactions are published online by the Ministry of Justice.

LAND ADMINISTRATION CHALLENGES

The overall performance of country-level land administration systems varies significantly. The GCC countries are the top performers, whereas most other countries are facing significant challenges. Those challenges have been measured by the World Bank's Doing Business indicators, which assessed various dimensions of the Quality of Land Administration indicator across MENA countries.[10] The Registering Property index, an overarching composite index ranging between 0 and 100, assesses both the efficiency and the quality of a country's land administration system (see figure 2.4, box 2.3, and table 2.1).

Figure 2.4 Registering Property scores, by region and MENA country/economy, 2020

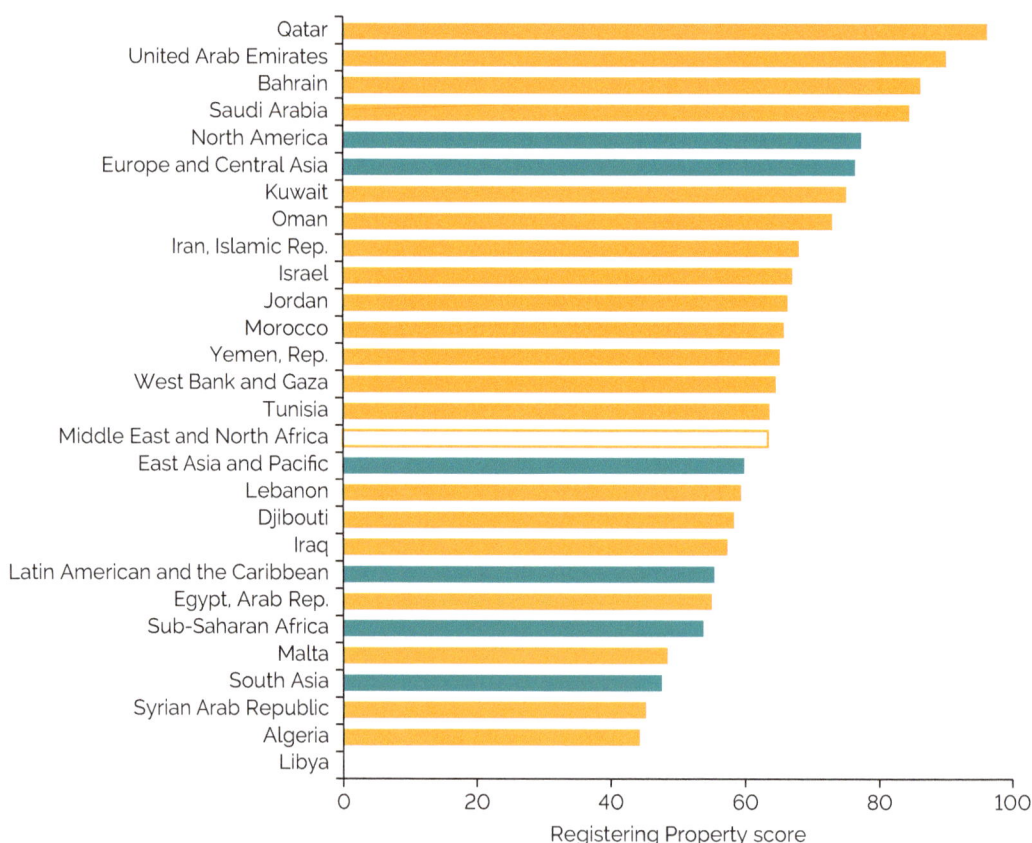

Source: World Bank, Doing Business 2004–2020 (database), https://archive.doingbusiness.org/en/doingbusiness.

In 2020, the MENA region received an average Registering Property score of 64.3, which was higher than the average score in Latin America and the Caribbean, East Asia and Pacific, South Asia, and Sub-Saharan Africa. This mean score, however, conceals a sharp contrast between the high scores received by many of the Gulf states, the very low scores of some MENA countries, and the middle-of-the-distribution scores received by others. The Gulf states lead the regional Doing Business rankings in Registering Property, with four states—Qatar (96.2), the United Arab Emirates (90.1), Bahrain (86.2), and Saudi Arabia (84.5)—also ranking in the top 20 globally (see figure 2.4). In fact, in 2020 Qatar ranked first in the world in the Registering Property index.[11] The MENA countries that rank at the bottom of the Registering Property index are conflict-affected countries such as Syria (45.2) and Iraq (57.3) and countries with large populations such as Algeria (44.3) or Egypt (55). These rankings could reflect the difficulty of setting up and maintaining comprehensive, up-to-date, transparent land administration systems in such contexts. Surprisingly, the Republic of Yemen (65.2) has an average score above the regional average.[12]

Box 2.3 Components of the Registering Property index

The Registering Property index rankings are determined by composite scores calculated using four equally weighted parts:

1. The number of procedures required to legally purchase and transfer property between parties
2. The time, in days, needed to purchase and transfer the property to be registered
3. The cost, recorded as a percentage of the property value, of transferring property between two parties, including transfer taxes or additional fees
4. The composite Quality of Land Administration index score.

Doing Business indicators primarily survey conditions in each country's main and secondary cities, and therefore they may not be completely representative of conditions in the country at large. For example, the Doing Business indicators do not consider residential and agricultural land in assessing the quality of land administration.

Source: World Bank, Doing Business 2004–2020 (database), https://archive.doingbusiness.org/en/doingbusiness.

Table 2.1 Registering Property index rankings, MENA, 2020

Country/economy	Registering Property rank	Registering Property score	Number of procedures	Time (days)	Cost (% of property value)	Quality of Land Administration (0–30)
Qatar	1	96.2	1	1	0.3	26.0
United Arab Emirates	10	90.1	2	1.5	0.2	21.0
Bahrain	17	86.2	2	2	1.7	19.5
Saudi Arabia	19	84.5	2	1.5	0.0	14.0
Kuwait	45	75.1	7	17	0.5	18.5
Oman	52	73.0	3	18	6.0	17.0
Iran, Islamic Rep.	70	68.1	6	31	3.8	16.0
Israel	75	67.1	6	37	7.2	22.5
Jordan	78	66.4	6	17	9.0	22.5

Continued

Table 2.1 **Registering Property index rankings, MENA, 2020** *(continued)*

Country/economy	Registering Property rank	Registering Property score	Number of procedures	Time (days)	Cost (% of property value)	Quality of Land Administration (0–30)
Morocco	81	65.8	6	20	6.4	17.0
Yemen, Rep.	86	65.2	6	19	1.8	7.0
West Bank and Gaza	91	64.6	7	35	3.0	13.5
Tunisia	94	63.7	5	35	6.1	13.5
Lebanon	110	59.4	8	37	6.0	16.0
Djibouti	117	58.3	6	24	5.6	7.0
Iraq	121	57.3	5	51	7.3	10.5
Egypt, Arab Rep.	130	55.0	9	76	1.1	9.0
Syrian Arab Republic	162	45.2	4	48	28	8.5
Algeria	165	44.3	10	55	7.1	7.5
Libya	187	0.0	—	—	—	—
MENA average	—	*64.3*	*5.3*	*28.7*	*5.2*	*15.1*

Source: World Bank, Doing Business 2004–2020 (database), https://archive.doingbusiness.org/en/doingbusiness.
Note: — = not applicable or not available.

In terms of the overall quality of land administration services, the smaller GCC countries also lead in the region, along with Jordan, which has made notable progress. The Quality of Land Administration index–a subindex of the Registering Property index (see figure 2.5 and table 2.2)–ranges between 0 and 30 and measures the reliability, transparency, and coverage of land administration, as well as the protection against land disputes and equal access to property rights. These criteria are measured by the five separate, subsidiary indexes presented in box 2.4. Table 2.2 is a breakdown of MENA countries' Quality of Land Administration scores by each index. Once again, Qatar leads the region in its overall Quality of Land Administration, with a score of 26, placing it in the top 20 in the world, with the same score as the United Kingdom, for example. Qatar achieved this improvement by publishing its official service standards and court statistics on land disputes.[13] Jordan has also made considerable progress regarding this indicator, ranking second in the MENA region, with a score of 22.5, which puts it in the top 50 with the same score as Israel and Spain. The smaller Gulf states (such as the United Arab Emirates, Bahrain, and Kuwait) also lead the region in Quality of Land Administration. However, Saudi Arabia, with a score of 14, slips below the regional average of 15.1. Conflict-affected states such as Syria (8.5) and the Republic of Yemen (7.0), countries with opaque institutions such as Algeria (7.5), and the poorest countries such as Djibouti (7.0) lag the other MENA countries, with Djibouti and the Republic of Yemen dropping to last place.

Figure 2.5 Quality of Land Administration indexes, by region and MENA country/economy, 2020

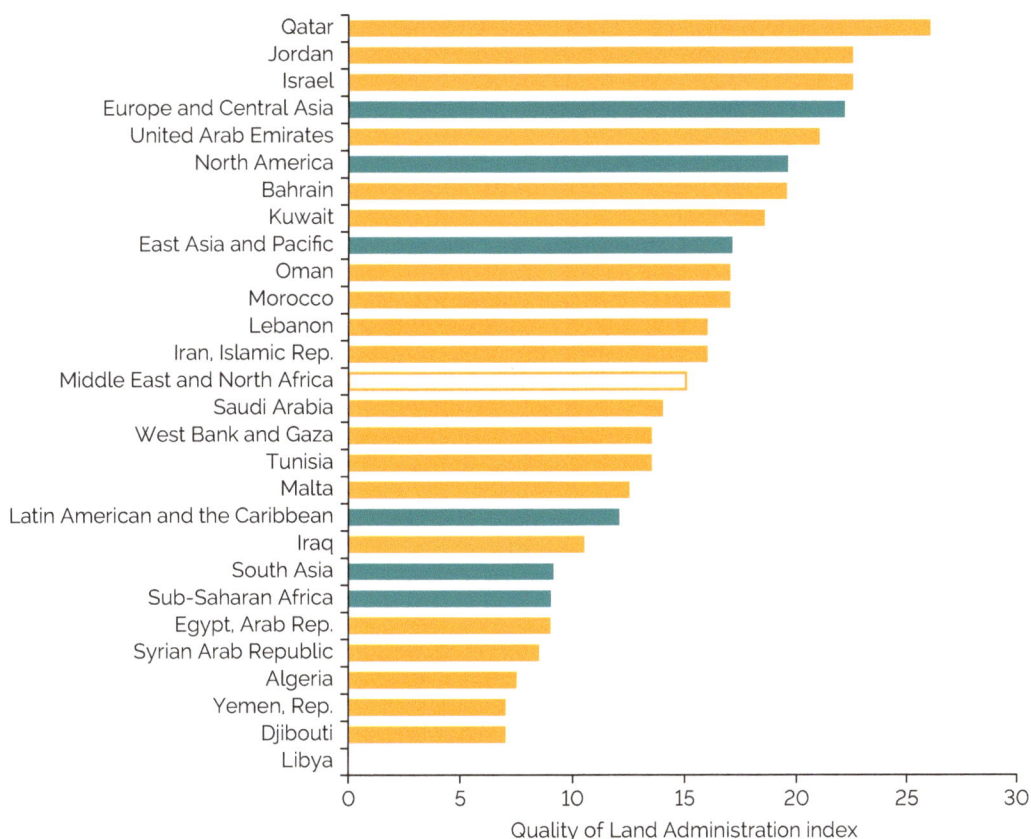

Source: World Bank, Doing Business 2004–2020 (database), https://archive.doingbusiness.org/en/doingbusiness.

Table 2.2 Quality of Land Administration index scores, MENA, 2020

Country/economy	Reliability of Infrastructure index (0–8)	Transparency of Information index (0–6)	Geographic Coverage index (0–8)	Land Dispute Resolution index (0–8)	Equal Access to Property Rights index (–2–0)	Total (0–30)
Qatar	8	3.5	8	6.5	0	26.0
Jordan	7	3.5	6	6.0	0	22.5
Israel	8	4.5	4	6.0	0	22.5
United Arab Emirates	8	2.5	4	6.5	0	21.0
Bahrain	6	3.5	4	6.0	0	19.5
Kuwait	3	2.5	8	5.0	0	18.5
Morocco	7	2.5	2	5.5	0	17.0
Oman	5	2.5	4	5.5	0	17.0
Iran, Islamic Rep.	6	1.0	4	5.0	0	16.0
Lebanon	4	3.0	4	5.0	0	16.0
Saudi Arabia	5	2.5	0	6.5	0	14.0

Continued

Table 2.2 Quality of Land Administration index scores, MENA, 2020 *(continued)*

Country/economy	Reliability of Infrastructure index (0–8)	Transparency of Information index (0–6)	Geographic Coverage index (0–8)	Land Dispute Resolution index (0–8)	Equal Access to Property Rights index (–2–0)	Total (0–30)
Tunisia	4	4.5	0	5.0	0	13.5
West Bank and Gaza	5	1.0	4	3.5	0	13.5
Iraq	1	0.5	4	5.0	0	10.5
Egypt, Arab Rep.	2	3.0	0	4.0	0	9.0
Syrian Arab Republic	2	2.5	0	4.0	0	8.5
Algeria	1	1.5	0	5.0	0	7.5
Djibouti	3	1.5	0	2.5	0	7.0
Yemen, Rep.	1	2.5	0	3.5	0	7.0
Libya	—	—	—	—	—	—
MENA average	*4.5*	*2.6*	*2.9*	*5.1*	*0*	*15.1*

Source: World Bank, Doing Business 2004–2020 (database), https://archive.doingbusiness.org/en/doingbusiness.
Note: — = not available.

Box 2.4 Components of the Quality of Land Administration index

The Quality of Land Administration index is a composite of five subsidiary indexes, each of which can be broken down into distinct components. These five indexes and an overview of the components they measure are as follows:

- The *Reliability of Infrastructure index* ranges from 0 to 8, with "higher values indicating a higher quality of infrastructure for ensuring the reliability of information on property titles and boundaries." Scores of 0, 1, or 2 are awarded for its six components. Most of these components pertain to the digitization and storage of land administration information, including formal land title certificates and cadastral plans.
- The *Transparency of Information index* ranges from 0 to 6, with "higher values indicating greater transparency in the land administration system." Scores of 0, 0.5, or 1 are awarded for its 10 components. Most of these components assess whether information on land ownership and property transactions are made easily accessible to the public.
- The *Geographic Coverage index* ranges from 0 to 8, with "higher values indicating greater geographic coverage in land ownership registration and cadastral mapping." A score of either 0 or 2 is awarded for its four components. These components address the completeness of land registry and mapping at the level of the largest business city and at the level of the economy.
- The *Land Dispute Resolution index* ranges from 0 to 8 and "assesses the legal framework for immovable property registration and the accessibility of dispute resolution mechanisms." Scores from 0 to 3 are awarded for its eight components. These components cover a variety of legal measures that pertain to the formal registration of land and dispute resolution processes.
- The *Equal Access to Property Rights index* ranges from –2 to 0, essentially penalizing countries' scores if there is a high degree of unequal access to property rights. Only two components are measured by this index: whether married men and married women have equal access, and whether unmarried men and unmarried women have equal access. If there is differential treatment in either case, a score of –1 is awarded.

The scores derived from the components outlined by these five indexes are then added, giving the overall Quality of Land Administration score.

Source: World Bank, Doing Business 2004–2020 (database), https://archive.doingbusiness.org/en/doingbusiness.

Generally, the quality of land administration services is greater in wealthier and smaller countries in the MENA region, possibly due to higher capacity or a limited number of transactions that exert less pressure on land administration systems.[14] For MENA countries, this is illustrated by the positive slope in panel a of figure 2.6, which plots the Quality of Land Administration score against GDP per capita, and by the negative slope in panel b, which plots the Quality of Land Administration score against population.[15]

Generally, GCC countries have in place well-performing registration systems, but lack of transparency of information remains an issue. Most other MENA countries face challenges related to the reliability and coverage of their registration systems in addition to a lack of transparency. The Reliability of Infrastructure index reflects these discrepancies, with an average score for MENA countries of only 4.5 (out of 8). Nine countries–Lebanon, Tunisia, Kuwait, Iraq, Djibouti, Egypt, Syria, Algeria, and the Republic of Yemen–score below the regional average (see box 2.4 and table 2.2). At the top of the ranking, one finds countries such as Qatar and the United Arab Emirates (with a maximum score of 8), both of which maintain formal land certificates and cadastral mapping plans in a fully digital format. As for the Transparency of Information index, no state in the MENA region scores higher than 4.5 out of 6, with the vast majority scoring below 3. In fact, only five countries in the whole region scored above the Doing Business global average for transparency of land information.

The geographic coverage of land registration is very problematic and sorely lacking in most MENA countries. This situation is captured by the Geographic Coverage index, which ranges from 0 to 8 and measures whether all plots of land have been registered and mapped at the level of the largest business city and in the economy as a whole. As shown in figure 2.7, only Jordan, Kuwait, and Qatar receive a score of 6 or more, whereas nine countries–Algeria, Djibouti, Egypt, Libya, Malta, Saudi Arabia, Syria, Tunisia, and the Republic of Yemen–receive a score of 0 (or "no practice" in the case of Libya). Among countries that receive a score of 2 or more, formal property registration and mapping are generally high at the level of the largest business city but tend to be lacking across the entire

Figure 2.6 Quality of Land Administration (QLA) scores, GDP per capita, and population, MENA

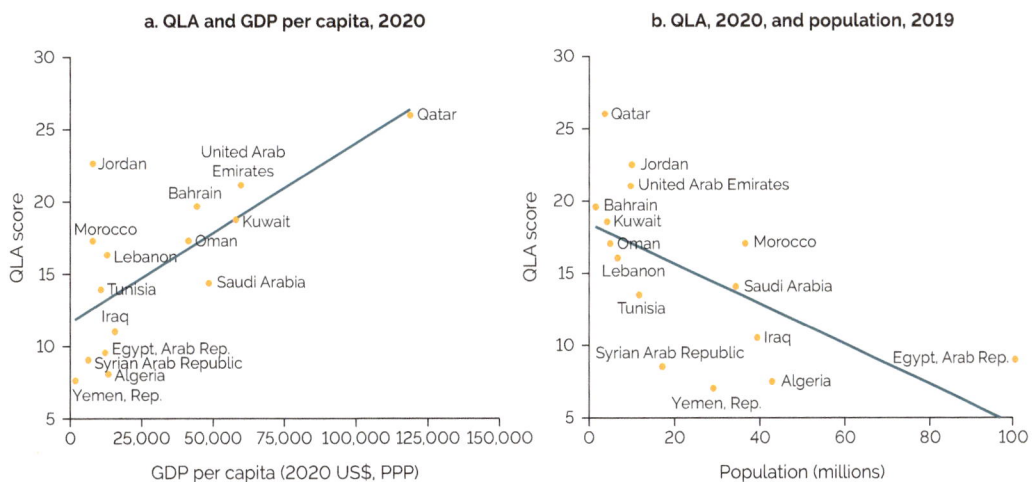

Sources: World Bank, Doing Business 2004–2020 (database), https://archive.doingbusiness.org/en/doingbusiness; World Bank, World Development Indicators (database), 2019, https://databank.worldbank.org/source/world-development-indicators.
Note: PPP = purchasing power parity.

Figure 2.7 Geographic Coverage scores, MENA, 2020

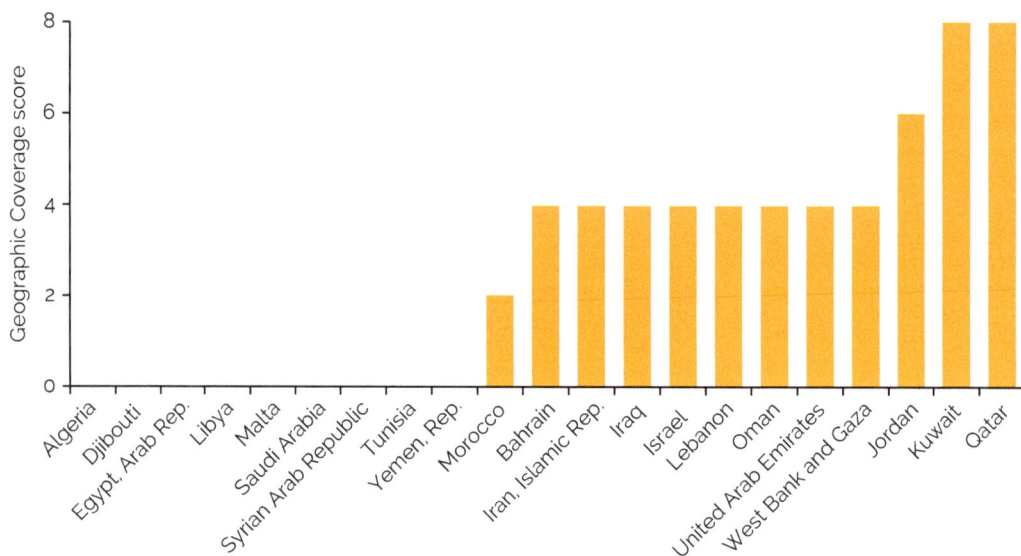

Source: World Bank, Doing Business 2004–2020 (database), https://archive.doingbusiness.org/en/doingbusiness.

economy. In the West Bank, for example, less than half of its land is formally registered. In Egypt, this figure is even lower–a mere 10 percent (World Bank 2018). In Lebanon, it is estimated that around 65 percent of all properties are surveyed and registered (Maarrawi 2020). Low levels of registration may be explained by several factors, including low demand for formal registration in the face of cumbersome and expensive regulatory procedures, lack of incentives to maintain formal property rights, lack of perception of benefits arising from formal tenure, lack of capacity of local governments to plan formal urban development that will contribute to widespread informal housing, and lack of clearly laid out processes to integrate customary rights into the statutory system.

Low levels of geographic coverage, in combination with lack of publicly available information and poor reliability of infrastructure, have likely contributed to a significant number of land-related disputes in some MENA countries. This is captured by the Doing Business Land Dispute Resolution index, which finds that the average legal framework for the resolution of property disputes scores 5.2 out of a possible 8, although procedures may not always be properly followed in practice, and national records to measure the prevalence of land disputes and efficiency of dispute resolution are generally not easily accessible.

Based on a study covering 16 countries (six of which are in the MENA region), the Justice Dashboard of the Hague Institute for Innovation of Law (HiiL) estimates that land disputes are among the most frequently cited legal problems (for 15 percent of respondents).[16] Another study on the West Bank and Gaza finds that 19 percent of all disputes recorded in Palestinian courts over a period of 50 years are land disputes (World Bank 2018). Similarly high figures have also been recorded in Algeria and Lebanon.

In these countries, disputes mainly concern competing claims of ownership–usually between private parties or with public authorities; inheritance issues; and property divisions. In many instances, these conflicts revolve around use of the power of attorney to transfer land. It is used as a substitute for paralyzed registration services, but it is often contested. Cases involving the division of property are often particularly cumbersome and may remain unresolved for years, resulting in assets undergoing improper transactions or being used inefficiently. Such issues are only further exacerbated by the fact that many MENA countries have relatively poor accessibility to dispute resolution mechanisms. For example, in the West Bank a proof of land ownership case usually takes up to 29 months to resolve and involves an average of five parties and 14 court hearings (World Bank 2018).

Ultimately, in the MENA region poor governance contributes to poor enforcement of property rights and high levels of tenure insecurity. The average Property Rights score from the Bertelsmann Transformation Index stands at 5.6 out of 10, which is only greater than that of South Asia and Sub-Saharan Africa.[17] Prindex, a global initiative that assesses the perception of land tenure security through comparable nationally representative surveys, finds that 28 percent of adults in the region consider it likely that they could lose their land or property against their will in the next five years—the highest percentage across regions.[18] Tenure insecurity in MENA countries is felt particularly in urban areas, among youth, among renters (especially those who do not have formal citizenship), and among women (see chapter 3).

NOTES

1. See Johnson and Ayachi (forthcoming) for more details on the historical development of land tenure systems in the MENA region.

2. Libya's Law 4/1978 on Real Property.

3. For example, a 1971 law conveyed *musha'* land that was owned by the state but not subjected to a right of collective use to municipalities, when such land was located within their borders.

4. State land and buildings are neither formally mapped nor registered through Iraq's immovable property registry. In the rare circumstances that public buildings are registered, there is often no indication of ownership or use rights.

5. Failure of the Ministry of Agriculture to develop these areas led to informal agricultural expansion by small-scale farmers.

6. Bertelsmann Stiftung, Bertelsmann Transformation Index (BTI) 2020 Country Reports, http://bti-project.org/.

7. BTI's Property Rights score measures the extent to which government authorities ensure that the rights of private property are well defined and regulate the acquisition, benefits, use, and sale of property. Analysis of the 2020 BTI Country Reports reveals the pervasive role of corruption, political interference, and cronyism in all MENA countries in private property rights. Transparency International's Corruption Perceptions Index (https://www.transparency.org/en/) measures the perceived public sector corruption using a scale of 0–100, where 0 is highly corrupt and 100 is free from corruption.

8. The GCC countries are Bahrain, Kuwait, Oman, Qatar, Saudi Arabia, and the United Arab Emirates.

9. A recent study of the West Bank (World Bank 2018) estimated that the effectiveness of property tax collection for unregistered land (1.8 percent) was less than half that for registered land (4.5 percent).

10. World Bank, Doing Business 2004–2020 (database), https://archive.doingbusiness.org/en/doingbusiness.

11. World Bank, Doing Business 2004–2020 (database), https://archive.doingbusiness.org/en/doingbusiness.

12. In the Republic of Yemen, there may be a large contrast between the capital city's average performance and that of the rest of the country, which is not captured in all subcomponent indicators. There are no data for Libya.

13. Qatar's score for Quality of Land Administration improved from 23.5 in 2016 to 26 in 2020.

14. Consistent with this observation, Doing Business reports that many Gulf states have a lower number of real estate transactions (World Bank 2020). An exception is Saudi Arabia.

15. By contrast, indicators of weaker land governance are generally associated with more informality, more poverty, and more inequality.

16. See https://dashboard.hiil.org/.

17. Bertelsmann Stiftung, Bertelsmann Transformation Index (BTI) 2020 Country Reports, MENA, http://bti-project .org/.

18. Prindex (dashboard), 2020, https://www.prindex.net/.

REFERENCES

Adamo, N., and N. Al-Ansari. 2020. "The First Century of Islam and the Question of Land and Its Cultivation (636–750 AD)." *Earth Sciences and Geotechnical Engineering* 10 (3): 137–58.

Balgley, D. 2015. "Morocco's Fragmented Land Regime: An Analysis of Negotiating and Implementing Land Tenure Policies." IPE Summer Research Grant Report, University of Puget Sound, Tacoma, WA. http://www .pugetsound.edu/files/resources/balgley.pdf.

Benessaiah, N. 2015. "Authority, Anarchy and Equity: A Political Ecology of Social Change in the Algerian Sahara." PhD diss., University of Kent, Kent, UK.

Coalition for Integrity and Accountability, AMAN. 2014. *Political Corruption in the Arab World.* Ramallah, West Bank: AMAN.

El-Meehy, A. 2013. "Institutional Development and Transition: Decentralization in the Course of Political Transformation." UNESCWA report, United Nations Economic and Social Commission for Western Asia, Beirut, Lebanon.

Foroudi, L. 2020. "'We Had to Get Our Land Back': Tunisian Date Farm Proves Revolutionary Bright Spot." Reuters, December 17, 2020. https://www.reuters.com/article/us-tunisia-uprising-land-idUSKBN28R0GH.

Hajrah, H. H. 1974. "Public Land Distribution in Saudi Arabia." PhD diss., Durham University, Durham, UK.

Hursh, J. 2014. "Women's Rights and Women's Land Rights in Postcolonial Tunisia and Morocco: Legal Institutions, Women's Rights Discourse, and the Need for Continued Reform." LLM diss., McGill University, Montreal, Quebec, Canada.

Johannsen, A., M. Nabil Mahrous, and M. Graversen. 2009. "Land-Owner Disputes in Egypt: A Case Study of the Abū Fānā Tensions in May 2008." *Arab West Report Paper,* No. 15, August 26, 2009.

Johnson, C., and N. Ayachi. Forthcoming. "Land Tenure Systems in the Middle East and North Africa Region: Historical Legacies from the 7th Century to the Present." Background paper prepared for this report, World Bank, Washington, DC.

Maarrawi, G. 2020. "The System of Land Registration in Lebanon." Presentation, Lebanese University Webinar, June 15–17, 2020, Beirut.

Nada, M., and D. Sims. 2020. "Assessment of Land Governance in Egypt." Background paper prepared for this report, World Bank, Washington, DC.

Palestinian National Authority. 2008. "National Land Policy Framework." Palestinian National Authority, Land Administration Project.

Puddephatt, A. 2012. "Corruption in Egypt." Global Partners and Associates, UK.

Revkin, M. R. 2014. "Triadic Legal Pluralism in North Sinai: A Case Study of State, Shari'a, and 'Urf Courts in Conflict and Cooperation." *UCLA Journal of Islamic and Near Eastern Law* 13: 21.

Sait, S., and H. Lim. 2006. *Land, Law and Islam: Property and Human Rights in the Muslim World.* London: Zed Books.

Salisu, T. M. 2013. "'Urf/'Adah (Custom): An Ancillary Mechanism in Shari'ah." *Ilorin Journal of Religious Studies* 3 (2): 133–48.

Unruh, J. 2016. "Mass Claims in Land and Property Following the Arab Spring: Lessons from Yemen." *Stability: International Journal of Security and Development* 5 (1).

USAID (US Agency for International Development). 2011. "Land Links: Morocco." https://www.land-links.org /country-profile/morocco/.

Waldner, D. 2004. "Land Code of 1858." In *Encyclopedia of the Modern Middle East and North Africa,* edited by P. Mattar. Detroit, MI: Thomson Gale. https://www.encyclopedia.com/humanities/encyclopedias-almanacs -transcripts-and-maps/land-code-1858.

World Bank. 2018. *Socio-Economic Effects of Weak Land Registration and Administration System in the West Bank.* Washington, DC: World Bank.

World Bank. 2020. *Doing Business 2020: Comparing Business Regulation in 190 Economies*. Washington, DC: World Bank. https://www.worldbank.org/en/programs/business-enabling-environment.

CHAPTER 3

Barriers to Accessing Land in the MENA Region

INTRODUCTION

This chapter illustrates how weaknesses in land governance, coupled with social norms and practices, restrict the access of both firms and individuals to land in the Middle East and North Africa (MENA), thereby hindering private sector development and contributing to exclusion and vulnerability.

FIRMS' DIFFICULTIES IN ACCESSING LAND

Barriers faced by firms in accessing land is a common problem in all MENA countries. Based on the World Bank's Enterprise Surveys, figure 3.1 shows the percentage of firms worldwide identifying access to land as a major or severe constraint to their business operations.[1] In the MENA region, firms' access to land is very difficult on average (23 percent), and only better than in Sub-Saharan Africa (29 percent). In seven of the ten MENA countries in the sample, more than 20 percent of firms face issues accessing land (more than 50 percent in Iraq).

Political connections likely facilitate access to land in MENA countries, where firms are more politically connected than in other regions (figure 3.2). Corporate political connection is a global but relatively more prevalent phenomenon in the MENA region. For example, there are twice as many politically connected firms in the MENA region (5.9 percent) as in the Europe and Central Asia (ECA) region (2.4 percent). The bulk of the politically connected firms in the MENA region are in Tunisia (27.9 percent) and Jordan (9.2 percent), exceeding the regional average of affected firms. Figure 3.3 presents the distribution of firms in the Arab Republic of Egypt, Morocco, and Tunisia, by political connection status, citing access to land as a major or severe constraint to their business operations. Clearly, in Morocco and Tunisia politically connected firms face fewer constraints in access to land than firms without political ties.

Figure 3.1 Firms finding access to land a major or severe constraint, by region and country/economy

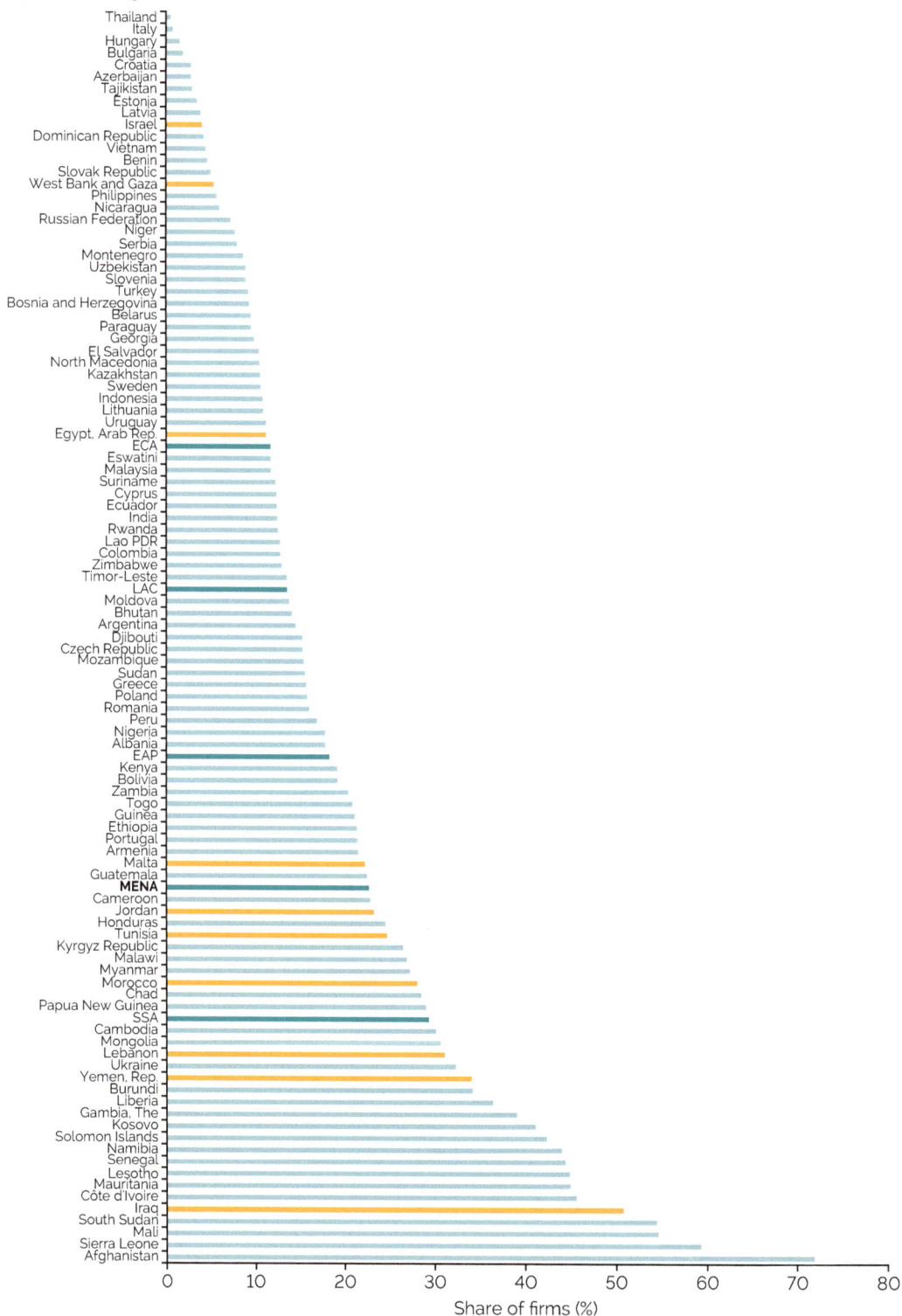

Source: Authors' calculations, based on World Bank, Enterprise Surveys (database), various years since 2013, https://www.enterprisesurveys.org/en/enterprisesurveys.

Note: This graph represents the percentage of manufacturing firms in each country (or economy) or region declaring in the World Bank Enterprise Surveys that access to land is a major or severe constraint in the current operations of the firm. EAP = East Asia and Pacific; ECA = Europe and Central Asia; LAC = Latin America and the Caribbean; MENA = Middle East and North Africa; SSA = Sub-Saharan Africa.

Figure 3.2 Share of politically connected firms, by region and MENA country/economy, 2019 and 2020

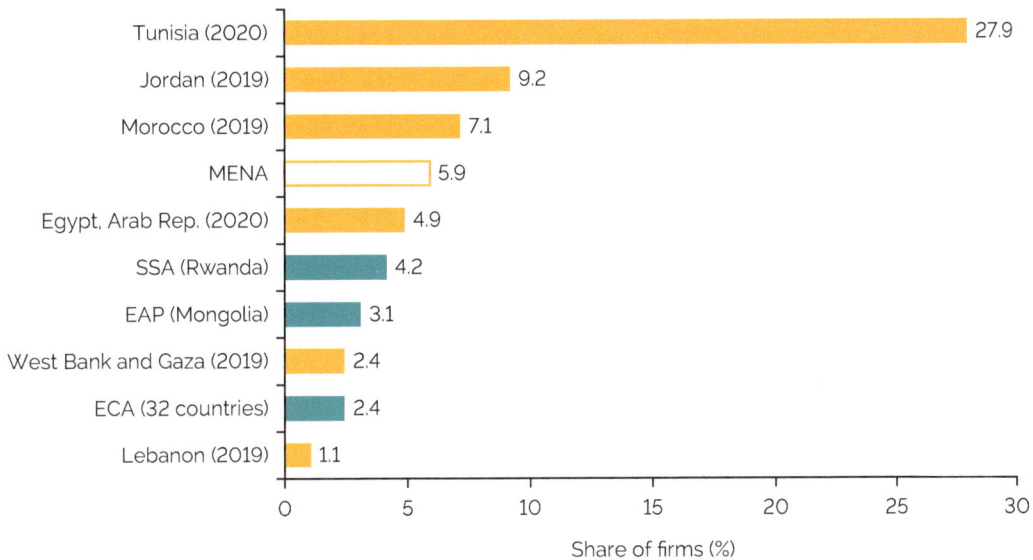

Source: World Bank, Enterprise Surveys (database), various years, https://www.enterprisesurveys.org/en/enterprisesurveys.
Note: The figure shows the share of politically connected firms in selected countries/economies and regions according to the World Bank's Enterprise Surveys. A respondent firm is reported as politically connected when any of its top officers (owner, CEO, top manager, or board member) has ever been elected or appointed to a political position. EAP = East Asia and Pacific; ECA = Europe and Central Asia; MENA = Middle East and North Africa; SSA = Sub-Saharan Africa.

Figure 3.3 Share of firms reporting severe constraints in access to land, by political connection status, the Arab Republic of Egypt, Morocco, and Tunisia, 2019 and 2020

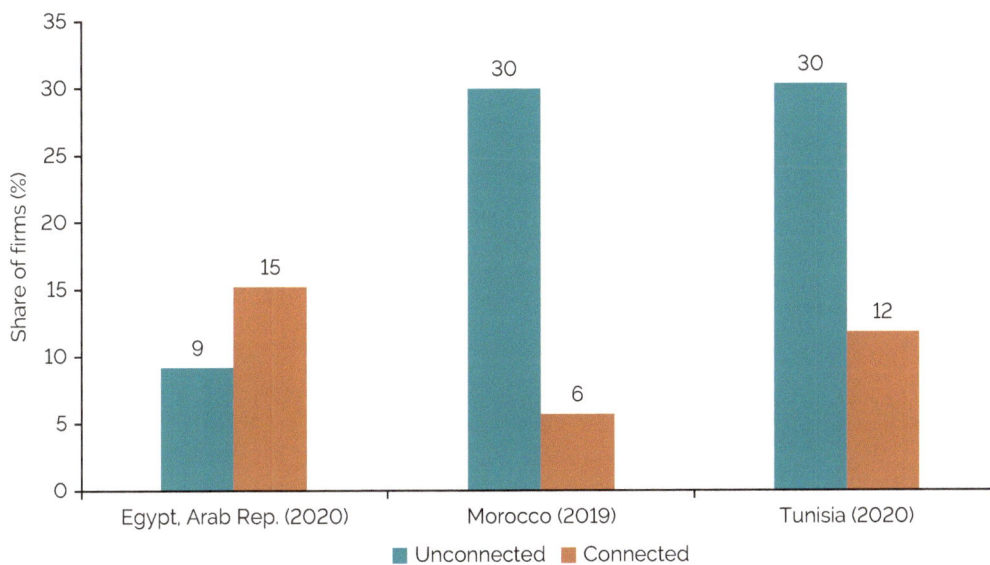

Source: World Bank, Enterprise Surveys (database), various years, https://www.enterprisesurveys.org/en/enterprisesurveys.

The value of political connections appears to be contingent on the existing political context and to be sensitive to political transitions. This pattern is assessed in a background paper prepared for this report based on the World Bank's Enterprise Surveys in Tunisia and Egypt (see annex 3A and Selod and Soumahoro, forthcoming). The study compares the difference in land access constraints faced by politically connected firms created after regime change (firms likely connected to the new regime) and politically connected firms created before regime change (firms whose political connections could have become obsolete) with the difference in land access constraints faced by politically unconnected firms created after and before regime change. The analysis indicates that active political connections likely helped reduce the share of firms facing severe constraints in accessing land by 20 percent in Egypt and 32 percent in Tunisia. The analysis also suggests that political connections with a former regime not only become less helpful but could even become detrimental to loosening land constraints after a political transition.

WOMEN'S DIFFICULTIES IN ACCESSING LAND

Women living in MENA countries continue to face a variety of difficulties in accessing land and protecting their land rights. This section describes gender discrepancies in access to land and property in the region and examines the ways in which formal and informal institutions perpetuate inequities between men and women.

According to scarce administrative data on registered properties, men in the MENA region own a much greater share of land and housing assets than women. Very few countries report or even calculate gender-disaggregated figures on land and housing ownership from their registries. Jordan is an exception; its Department of Land and Surveys maintains registration data by gender. In 2014, Jordanian women owned 24.7 percent of registered apartments, whereas men owned 70 percent, and the rest was co-owned by men and women (5.3 percent). However, such figures calculated from administrative data only reflect ownership disparities among the subset of properties that are formally registered. In fact, gender inequality in land and property ownership is likely significantly greater than the administrative figures suggest, and rates of female ownership of housing and land are probably even lower for unregistered properties.[2]

Overall, gender discrepancies in land and housing ownership are even starker in nationally representative surveys, which also cover nonregistered property.[3] Female ownership of land in Jordan's Population and Family Health Survey is much lower than that reported in 2012 by the Department of Land and Surveys, with roughly 7 percent of married women owning land (versus 51 percent of men) and 7 percent owning a house (versus 61 percent of men).[4] In Egypt, it is estimated that only 2 percent of married women between the ages of 15 and 49 own land, and only 5 percent own a house (Ministry of Health and Population, El-Zanaty and Associates, and ICF International 2015). A pilot survey undertaken for this report on inheritance in the West Bank and Gaza reveals that less than 20 percent of women owned land at the time of their death, compared with about half of men (World Bank 2019). When inquiring about residential property ownership, the survey displays an even more striking difference, with about 5 percent of women owning their home at the time of their passing, compared with 77 percent of men.[5] The same survey administered in rural areas in Tunisia finds that 21 percent of women owned land at the time of their death, compared with 87 percent of men (GIZ 2021).[6] Gender discrepancies in ownership also emerge in the Prindex surveys,[7] which find that in the MENA region men are twice as likely as women to be owners or joint owners of the property in which they reside.[8]

Gender gaps are often magnified in rural areas, with the MENA region having the lowest rate of women's agricultural land ownership in the world and with women holding smaller plots and facing greater restrictions to access finance for agricultural investments. Throughout the MENA region, it is estimated that only 5 percent of women own agricultural properties (despite 40 percent of women participating in agricultural production). This is the lowest rate of women's agricultural land ownership in the developing world, compared with 11 percent in Asia (excluding Japan), 15 percent in Sub-Saharan Africa, and 18 percent in Latin America (Campos et al. 2015; USAID 2016). In addition, in most MENA countries agricultural land plots owned by women are typically smaller and less productive than those owned by men (Lawry et al. 2017; World Bank 2011).[9] On many family farms, women are often not paid for their work, further increasing their vulnerability and economic dependency.[10] Sharecropping contracts are rarely signed by women, even though they obtained this fundamental right during agrarian reforms in Algeria, Egypt, and the Syrian Arab Republic in the 1950s. This finding may stem, in part, from women's low literacy rates–particularly among women living in rural areas–which prevents them from accessing information about land rights or from reading, understanding, and signing equitable contracts.[11] Similarly, female farmers face more restrictions than males in accessing finance (possibly exacerbated by their difficulty in using land as collateral).[12]

In addition to low ownership rates, women in the MENA region face higher tenure insecurity[13] than men, a gender discrepancy that is greater in MENA countries than in the rest of the world. Because women primarily gain access to land through marriage and inheritance, their vulnerability is evident in the case of divorce or the death of their spouse. Women may not be entitled to keep the land they worked on or owned, or they may be denied the right to inhabit their marital property or maintain an economic activity on agricultural land by their eldest son or brothers-in-law (see COHRE 2006). The global Prindex survey on land and property rights confirms this vulnerability by estimating the share of married women and married men who fear losing their land in the case of a divorce or spousal death.[14] Figure 3.4 shows these estimates for MENA economies, painting a clear picture of why women feel much less secure than men. In Egypt, in particular, 41 percent of women versus 4 percent of men worry about losing their property in the event of a divorce (see panel a of figure 3.4). A similar narrative emerges about losing property in the event of the death of a spouse. For example, 37 percent of women (versus 7 percent of men) in Morocco and 31 percent of women (versus 3 percent of men) in Egypt worry about this scenario (see panel b of figure 3.4). Overall, it is in the MENA region where married women compared with married men feel the greatest risk of losing property in these two scenarios. The discrepancy between the two is 21 percentage points (Prindex 2020).[15]

These discrepancies in ownership of land and property and in tenure security arise from formal and informal institutions that do not sufficiently support women's rights. Civil and religious laws that favor men in matters of inheritance and asset management and gender-imbalanced social norms and practices are two of the primary causes of inequity in land and property ownership throughout the MENA region. In most MENA countries, legal frameworks grant men and women comparable rights in a variety of matters. Under civil law, women can own, start, and sell a business; conduct financial deals; buy, sell, lease, and mortgage property; independently grant power of attorney; and much more. In many countries, however, legal frameworks continue to disadvantage women in two important ways: they deny women equal inheritance rights over land and property, and they disempower women in asset management.

Inheritance procedures in MENA countries follow various interpretations of Islamic law, but no country in the MENA region grants male and female children equal inheritance rights over assets. In both the Sunni and Shia religious schools, daughters receive half of their brother's share.[16] Furthermore, although it is notable that spouses inherit in Islam, the only country that grants spouses equal inheritance rights is the United Arab Emirates. In Sunni Islam, widows receive a quarter of the husband's estate if there are no heirs and only one-eighth if there are heirs. In Shia Islam, widows are not entitled to inherit land. Apart from Lebanon, Syria, and, to some extent, Egypt, religious minorities also apply *shari'a* principles to inheritance.[17] In fact, Christians and Muslims throughout the MENA region have adopted similar strategies for passing on control of land and property to male heirs. For example, Jordanian Christians seem to have willingly applied *shari'a* law to matters of inheritance in their own courts and tribunals for decades (see Jansen 1993; JNCW 2010).

Figure 3.4 **Gender differences in perceived tenure insecurity in the event of a divorce or death of spouse, MENA**

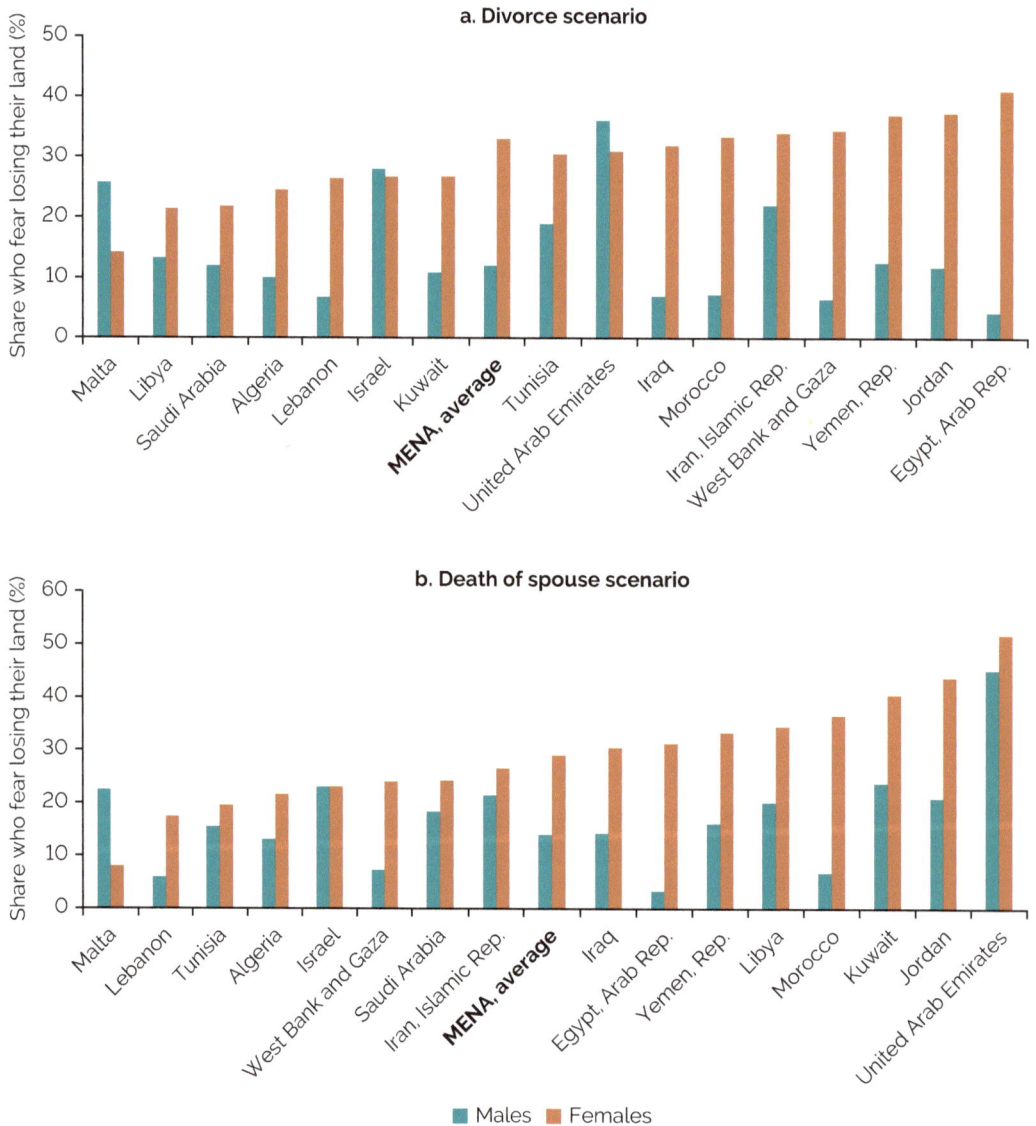

Source: Prindex (dashboard), 2020, https://www.prindex.net/.
Note: Panel a shows for each MENA country or economy the shares of married women and men who fear losing their land in a divorce; in panel b in the death of a spouse.

In many MENA countries, there are no legal provisions sanctioning the obstruction of women's access to their right of inheritance. However, the jurisprudential interpretation (*fiqh* in Arabic, *foqaha* in Farsi) of *shari'a* law is performed by men, and laws often lack sufficient enforcement mechanisms. As a result, men are not deterred from or held accountable for depriving women of their inherited assets (WCLAC 2014). Similarly, Islamic law does not specify a punishment in cases of noncompliance with inheritance subdivisions. Consequently, women are often prevented from receiving their due inheritance assets. For example, figure 3.5 shows that over the past 10 years, on average, about a quarter of inheritance court cases in Jordan are related to the exclusion of heirs. However, since 2011, when Jordan introduced legal protection from forced renunciation of inheritance, there has been an overall downward trend in this percentage (see figure 3.6). Other countries—such as Egypt in 2011—have also recently enacted legal provisions condemning any person who deliberately prevents heirs—primarily women—from receiving their share of inheritance (ECWR 2017). Nevertheless, exclusion of women in inheritance cases persists throughout the MENA region.

Figure 3.5 **Number of inheritance cases related to exclusion of heirs in *shari'a* courts, Jordan, 2010–20**

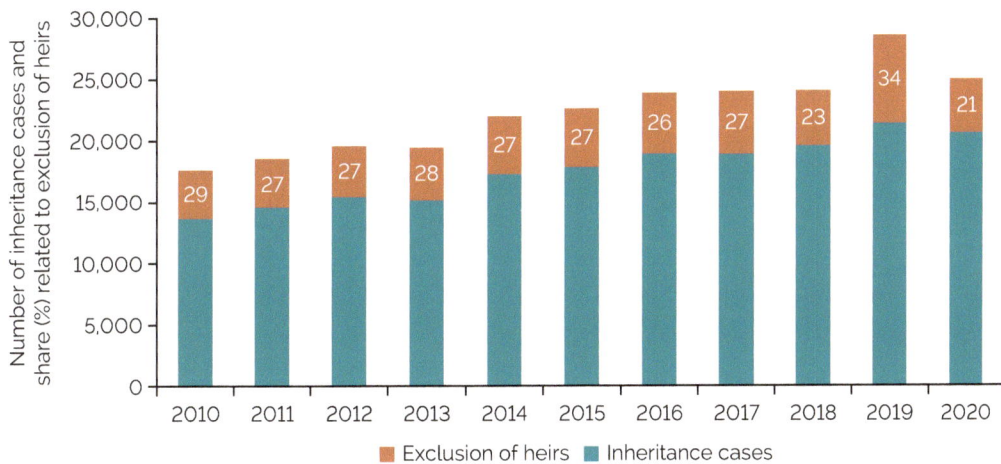

Source: Jordan *shari'a* courts, 2010–20.

Figure 3.6 **Evolution of the share of inheritance cases related to exclusion of heirs in *shari'a* courts, Jordan, 2010–20**

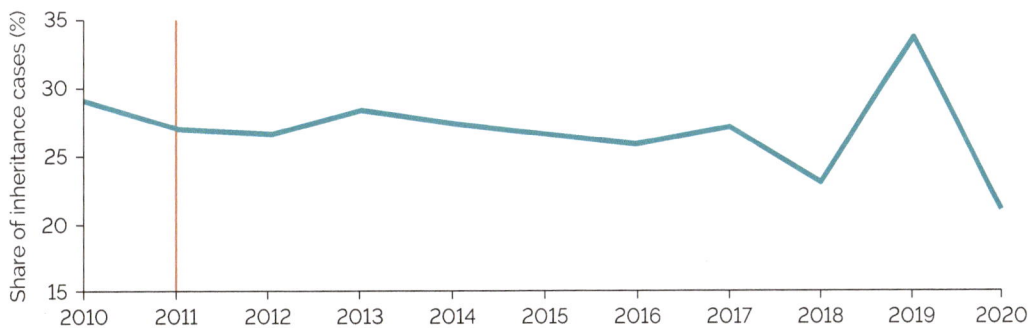

Source: Jordan *shari'a* courts, 2010–20.
Note: The vertical line marks the introduction of legal protection from forced renunciation of inheritance.

Discriminatory inheritance laws undermine women's economic security, particularly about asset management. Such inequity against women is highlighted by the World Bank's *Women, Business and the Law* (WBL) index, which identifies legal constraints to women's economic independence using eight indicators, including the Assets indicator, which assesses gender differences in property and inheritance.[18] On a global level, the WBL finds that the slowest pace of reforms toward equality of the sexes is in property and inheritance. Figure 3.7 illustrates how static reforms affecting the WBL's Assets indicator have been over the last 10 years. Although this is true for all regions, it is particularly true for MENA countries because such reforms are often seen as a challenge to the jurisprudence and social norms of *shari'a* law. In 10 countries surveyed by the Arab Barometer (2020), only in Lebanon did the majority of people believe that women's inheritance share should be equal to that of men. In addition to the slow pace of reforms, the MENA region has the lowest score for the management of assets. Women unduly suffer the consequences of such a stagnant pace of reforms to equality in asset management.

Throughout the MENA region, social norms exert strong pressure on women to renounce their inheritance rights over property, often without fair compensation. Traditionally, land has been considered an important source of income that enables men to take care of their family. Families are thus often reluctant to give land shares to female children who, once married, will pass valuable assets to their husband's family.

For decades, women have been excluded from inheritance through social pressure to voluntarily renounce their rights in favor of their brothers—a practice known as *takharruj*. Although data on this practice are scarce, Jordanian *shari'a* court data reveal that in 2014 a third of heirs fully relinquished their inheritance rights through *takharruj*. In the West Bank and

Figure 3.7 Gender equality in legal frameworks governing property and inheritance, by region, 1970–2020

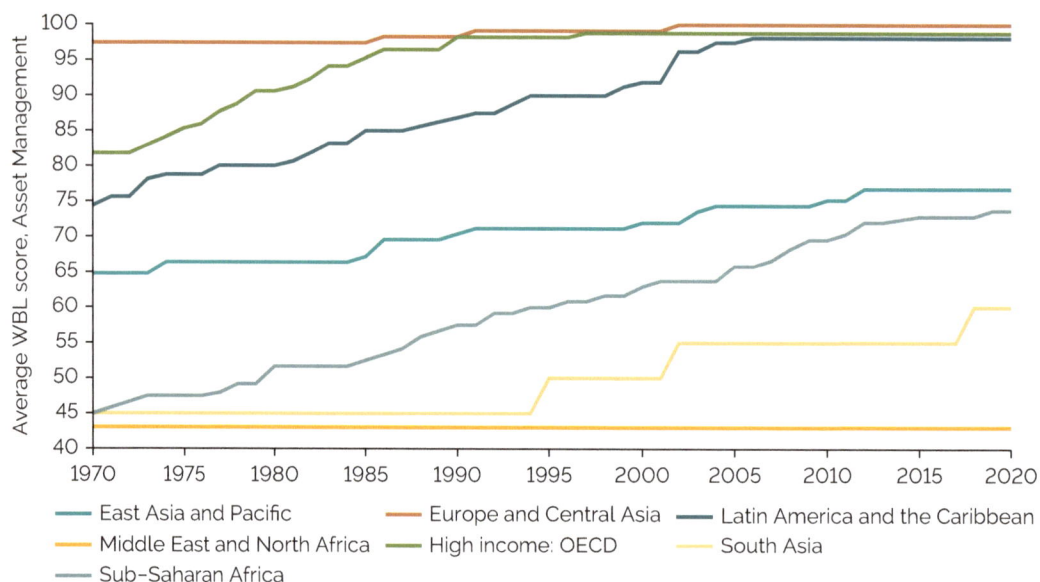

Source: Authors' calculations, based on the Assets indicator in *Women, Business and the Law 2020* (World Bank 2020).
Note: OECD = Organisation for Economic Co-operation and Development; WBL = *Women, Business and the Law.*

Gaza, the pilot survey conducted for this report (World Bank 2019) indicates that 16 percent of women renounced their shares in favor of others when inheriting a residential property, and that 28 percent of women eligible to inherit land did not receive their fair share and were insufficiently or not at all compensated. In Tunisia, replication of the pilot in the rural areas of eight regions showed that more than 70 percent of women eligible to inherit land did not receive their share (GIZ 2021).[19] In Egypt, it is estimated that nearly 60 percent of women are denied their inheritance shares, with the practice of *takharruj* particularly prevalent throughout Upper Egypt (Najjar, Baruah, and El Garhi 2020).

Discriminatory social norms also prevent women from asserting their rights in court. Women who refuse to waive their inheritance rights are often threatened with abandonment, ostracism, and, in extreme cases, verbal abuse and physical violence (Naffa et al. 2007). Significant pressure may be exerted to deter women who have been cheated or disagree about the division of inheritance property from seeking justice through the legal system. Social norms condemn anyone bringing a lawsuit against a family member. Furthermore, pursuing a legal claim to inheritance is costly and difficult for women if male family members are reluctant to cooperate (Prettitore 2013a, 2013b). In a 2017 report on public perceptions of Palestinian justice and security institutions, the United Nations Development Programme (UNDP) found that Palestinian women are often very reluctant to go to court and are generally less likely than men to utilize justice and security institutions (UNDP 2017).[20] Finally, a survey carried out in 2009 by the Women's Affairs Center in Gaza found that 23.8 percent of women were denied their right to inheritance, and 62.5 percent did not receive any kind of external legal advice (NRC 2011).

Women may also be deprived of their inheritance through channels other than explicit renunciation. These channels include avoidance of land subdivision, sales to male relatives prior to the implementation of inheritance procedures, lack of property registration, or incomplete disclosure of the assets in the deceased's estate. In many countries in the region, the most common of these techniques is forestalling the subdivision of land—sometimes over decades—to prevent land fragmentation,[21] which has a negative impact on women's ability to gain control and benefit from properties. For example, a 2010 survey by the Jordanian National Forum for Women found that the principal method employed to deprive women of their rights is to obstruct the division of inheritance between heirs. The study revealed that 34 percent of women residing in the Irbid governorate did not receive their legal share of inheritance because of the absence of land division (Ababsa 2017).[22]

Another common practice in Jordan is the donation of land to male heirs before the father's death. Donations are registered as sales and encouraged by the 1 percent tax that applies (versus a 9 percent tax when land is sold outside of the family). Often, women are kept in the dark about the real value of donated assets, and so male heirs may give symbolic gifts to women as a form of compensation–called *qa* or *takrim* in Jordan–which are worth far less than the value of shares they are legally entitled to inherit. In Jordan, according to data from the Department of Land and Surveys prepared for Ababsa (2017), more than a third (37 percent) of land transactions in 2014 were conducted between close relatives (*usūl wa-fughūr*)—that is, between parents and children, between siblings, between husband and wife. Most transactions appear to be between fathers and sons, or fathers and their brothers, but not involving women. In fact, over the years the number of land sales within the family unit has been trending upward: from a quarter of the sales in 2005 to more than a third in 2014.

Poor access to land and property, together with other gender imbalances, likely has detrimental impacts on the economic status of women and negative impacts on economic development throughout the MENA region. Generally, in the MENA region—and in the rest of the world—countries with high levels of gender inequality also tend to have the poorest-quality land administration (see figure 3.8). However, it is difficult to gauge the true impact of discrepancies in land ownership and tenure insecurity on women's economic outcomes because empirical evidence is sorely lacking for most MENA countries. Nevertheless, research undertaken in other regions and the barriers to accessing land faced by women in the MENA region suggest that there is a variety of detrimental consequences of gender differences in land accessibility (Meinzen-Dick et al. 2019). For example, without land and property women may not be able to borrow money using land as collateral. They then cannot diversify their livelihood opportunities by, for example, starting an agri-processing business.

Limiting income generation for women in this way may contribute to household poverty, especially for widows or divorced women. Moreover, women's limited access to land and rights over land limits, in turn, their decision-making within households. And it has negative impacts on their empowerment vis-à-vis their spouses, as well as intergenerational consequences because women may not be able to provide adequate nutrition or education for their children. Furthermore, the entire economy suffers from foregone investment because of weak land rights for women. Property rights and security of tenure are thus essential for the improvement of livelihoods, economic prosperity, and sustainable development.[23]

Figure 3.8 Gender inequality and quality of land administration, MENA and rest of the world

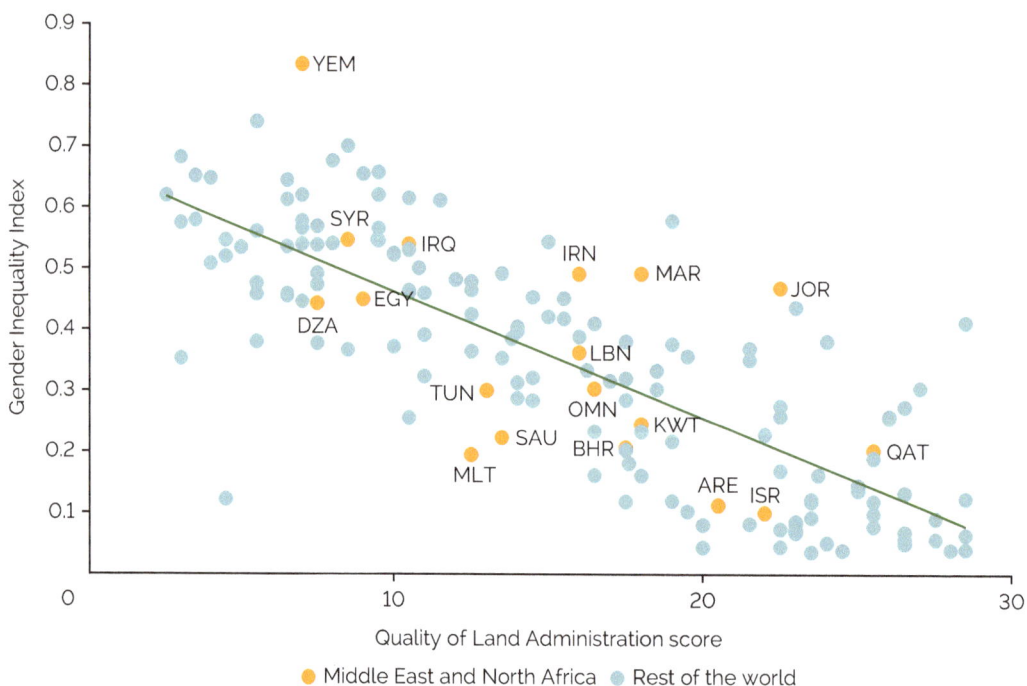

Sources: Quality of Land Administration score: World Bank, Doing Business 2004–2020 (database), https://archive.doingbusiness.org/en/doingbusiness; Gender Inequality Index: UNDP (2018).
Note: In the graph, the horizontal and vertical axes provide the 2020 scores for the Quality of Land Administration index and the Gender Inequality Index, respectively. For country codes, see figure 1.4.

REFUGEES, INTERNALLY DISPLACED PERSONS, AND THEIR LAND AND PROPERTY RIGHTS

This section describes the difficulties that refugees and internally displaced persons (IDPs) face throughout the MENA region in accessing land and protecting land rights.

Conflicts in the MENA region have pushed the housing, land, and property (HLP) rights of refugees and IDPs front and center as a key issue to be addressed for reconstruction and recovery.[24] Conflicts and the resulting population displacements have given rise to the need for urgent legislative reforms, including support for refugees' and IDPs' access to land and housing in destination areas, legal protections for land and property assets, and dispute resolution mechanisms for forced sales, abandoned properties, and destruction of property documents in origin areas.

Destruction of property rights documentation and lack of transparent land registries and conflicting systems of tenure complicate the current national reconciliation process, including provisions for compensation and restitution of property. The recent wars in Iraq, Libya, Syria, and the Republic of Yemen have caused immense suffering and destruction, displacing millions of refugees and IDPs. The majority do not possess any reliable proof of ownership of their properties, and, if they do, it is often destroyed or confiscated. For example, in southern Syria only 9 percent of internally displaced families have retained their property deeds (NRC 2017). The confiscation of HLP documentation from refugees and IDPs is a way to deprive them of the ability to reclaim their property and to return (Vignal 2019). In Syria, 7 million Syrian refugees and 6 million internally displaced Syrians have been deprived of their basic rights to housing and property.

In 2018, the Syrian government enacted Law no. 10, which expanded the controversial 2012 Decree no. 66. Law no. 10 gives millions of refugees only 30 days to return and claim their property rights in urban areas (Yahya 2018). In addition, several registry offices have been burned down—primarily in Homs, but also in Membij, Zabadani, Daraya, and Al-Qusayr—to prevent formal owners from claiming their rights. Often, IDPs and refugees, fearing arrest by local authorities, may be unable to access local registration offices to reconstitute their documentation. The war in the Republic of Yemen has led to land grabbing and tribal claims, in particular in the provinces of al-Hudayda (west), Lahij (south), and Sa'da (north). The absence of a transparent land registry and conflicting systems of tenure complicate the current national reconciliation process, including provisions for compensation and restitution of property (Unruh 2016). Addressing the tenure rights of refugees is particularly sensitive when the issue is property restitution or eviction of secondary occupants. These situations require formulating new provisions for the current legal frameworks or revising existing provisions that are not in line with international law.

History has shown that unresolved land disputes may otherwise become a catalyst for conflict between opposing groups. For example, in 1950 Israel promulgated the Absentee Property Law and applied it to the land of 760,000 Palestinians who were expelled between December 1947 and September 1949. This law led to the confiscation of 60 percent of what was Palestinian rural land, or 3,250 square kilometers of agricultural land (Benvenisti and Zamir 1995). In 1973, an Absentees' Property (Compensation) Law was enacted by the Israeli government, which gave Israeli citizenship to Palestinian residents, mostly in the eastern part of Jerusalem, who were until then considered absentees. However, the sums offered as compensation were not adequate because they were based on the pre-1948 land prices (Benvenisti and Zamir 1995).

In several destination countries, refugees are not allowed to purchase land and property, which increases their vulnerability and contributes to informality in urban and peri-urban areas. For example, 450,000 Palestinian refugees have been denied the right to own property in Lebanon by means of Law 296 of 2001 (OHCHR 2021). It was not until 2018 that Gazan refugees (who were not Jordanian citizens) were allowed to buy land or property in Jordan (*Al-Monitor* 2018; *Jordan Times* 2018), unlike the 2.2 million Palestinian refugees registered at the United Nations Relief and Works Agency for Palestine Refugees in the Near East (UNRWA) (who are Jordanian citizens). Furthermore, competition over land in host urban areas increases with the influx of refugees and displaced persons. Because of weak land administration services, this phenomenon exacerbates informality and promotes parallel (informal) systems for registration and dispute resolution. In Lebanon, for example, Palestinian refugees have been using parallel systems to administer land transactions in refugee camps (World Bank, forthcoming).

International organizations have provided guidelines to support recognition and protection of refugees' land, housing, and property rights. In August 2005, the United Nations adopted the Pinheiro Principles on Housing and Property Restitution for Refugees and Displaced Persons. The principles provide practical guidance for governments, international organizations, and nongovernmental organizations seeking to restore HLP rights after violent conflicts (UNESC 2005). They are designed to facilitate the return of refugees to their homes by restoring the status quo ante bellum of housing, land, and property (Paglione 2008). Meanwhile, the Pinheiro Principles provide useful guidance on the international standards governing the effective implementation of housing, land, and property restitution programs and mechanisms. Two years later, in 2007, the related *Handbook on Housing and Property Restitution for Refugees and Displaced Persons: Implementing the "Pinheiro Principles"* was published (FAO et al. 2007). It covers rights to housing and property restitution, equality between men and women, adequate housing, protection from displacement, and the right to return in safety and dignity. The document recommends that joint ownership rights for both male and female heads of household be an explicit component of the restitution process.[25]

ANNEX 3A: THE ROLE OF POLITICAL CONNECTIONS IN FACILITATING ACCESS TO LAND IN TUNISIA AND EGYPT

In undertaking background research for this report, Selod and Soumahoro (forthcoming) turned to the World Bank's Enterprise Surveys to investigate the value of political connections in facilitating firms' access to land in Egypt, Morocco, and Tunisia. In these countries, firms face constraints in accessing land (see figure 3.3 in chapter 3), and a portion of firms have political connections. The three countries present contrasting patterns. Connected firms (that is, those with elected or appointed top officers) in Morocco and Tunisia report fewer constraints in accessing land, but, paradoxically, those in Egypt face more constraints in accessing land (figure 3.3).

To explain this paradox, the authors further investigated whether the value of political connections in accessing land had been weakened or lost with regime change in Tunisia (in 2011) and in Egypt (in 2013). They distinguished between firms created before and after regime change in these two countries and then ran a regression that compares access to land before and after regime change for firms possibly not politically connected with the new regime (because they were created before regime change) and possibly connected with the new regime (because they were created after regime change).

Results from this difference-in-differences (DID) estimation are presented in table 3A.1 for Egyptian and Tunisian firms. Columns 1 and 2 report the shares of firms facing major or severe constraints in accessing land for the groups of firms created before and after regime change, respectively. Column 3 compares the averages in groups created before and after regime change, subtracting column 1 from column 2, for both politically connected (treated) and unconnected (control) firms. The DID subtracts the within-group difference for unconnected firms (row 2, column 3) from the within-group difference for connected firms (row 1, column 3), thereby adjusting for the fact that the two types of firms were not the same at baseline.

Clearly, the value of political connections appears to be contingent on the existing political context in the MENA region. In Egypt, the policy environment under the new regime helped reduce the shares of politically connected firms that were severely land-constrained by 20 percent relative to unconnected firms. Perhaps this is the source of the paradox in figure 3.3, suggesting that old political connections were not helpful or became detrimental in reducing land constraints in Egypt. In Tunisia, the share of politically connected firms created just after the Arab Spring facing severe constraints in access to land dropped by about 32 percent relative to unconnected firms. Together, these results indicate that the gains from corporate political connections are likely to be tied to a specific political context and therefore may be sensitive to political transition.

Table 3A.1 Effects of regime change on land access constraints, the Arab Republic of Egypt and Tunisia

Country	(1) Firms created before regime change	(2) Firms created after regime change	(3) Within-group difference [(2) – (1)]
Egypt, Arab Rep.			
1. Connected (treated)	.224	.077	–.147* (.090)
2. Unconnected (control)	.098	.152	.053*** (.019)
3. Difference-in-differences			**–.201** (.092)**
Tunisia			
1. Connected (treated)	.240	.050	–.190* (.116)
2. Unconnected (control)	.380	.514	.134** (.062)
3. Difference-in-differences			**–.324** (.131)**

Source: World Bank, Enterprise Surveys (database), https://www.enterprisesurveys.org/en/enterprisesurveys.
*$p < 0.1$; **$p < 0.05$; ***$p < 0.01$.

NOTES

1. World Bank, Enterprise Surveys (database), https://www.enterprisesurveys.org/en/enterprisesurveys.

2. In Jordan, registered apartments owned by women are estimated to represent only 10.3 percent of all apartments irrespective of registration status (Department of Statistics, Jordan, Population and Housing 2015 [dashboard], http://dosweb.dos.gov.jo/censuses/population_housing/census2015/; Hamilton et al. 2018).

3. Surveys may not, however, distinguish between registered and nonregistered property.

4. Department of Statistics, Jordan, Population and Family Health Survey 2012, https://microdata.worldbank.org/index.php/catalog/1908.

5. The survey was carried out in June 2019 in rural and urban areas of the West Bank and Gaza of a sample of 581 randomly selected women. It focused on inheritance issues. Thus the reported figures on land and residential properties of mothers and fathers are *at the time of their death*. Asset ownership rates are likely greater at later stages in life.

6. The survey uses the same questionnaire as the West Bank and Gaza pilot (with minor adaptations). It was administered by the Deutsche Gesellschaft für Internationale Zusammenarbeit (GIZ) in Tunisia's rural areas in October 2020 and covers a sample of 509 women from eight regions.

7. See Prindex (dashboard), 2020, https://www.prindex.net/.

8. Authors' calculation from Prindex data in 16 MENA countries using population-weighted averages. Prindex (dashboard), 2020, https://www.prindex.net/.

9. In Egypt, Morocco, and Tunisia, there is a direct inverse correlation between farm size and women's involvement in agricultural activities: the larger the farm, the fewer women involved. Conversely, the smaller the farm, the greater the responsibility of women.

10. For example, a study reports that in Tunisia, although women provide 80 percent of the labor on family farms, they are usually not paid (FAO/IFAD 2007). An earlier study by Christensen, Veillerette, and Andricopulos (2007) found large percentages of unpaid female workers in the Republic of Yemen (79 percent), Syrian Arab Republic (66 percent), Egypt (60 percent), and the West Bank and Gaza (45 percent). This is a broad trend in the MENA region, where less than one woman out of four is engaged in a paid activity, and where the female labor participation rate, at 25.2 percent, is the lowest in the world (World Bank 2013).

11. In Morocco, for example, two-thirds of rural women and one-third of urban women are illiterate (Haut Commissariat au Plan 2019). In Egypt, 30.8 percent of women are illiterate versus 21.1 percent of men (CAPMAS 2020).

12. In Jordan, only 21 percent of women who are head of household receive loans for agricultural development, and 9 percent receive loans for income-generating activities. The respective rates for male heads of household are 43 percent and 14 percent (IFAD 2013).

13. Tenure insecurity is the risk of losing one's land.

14. Prindex (dashboard), 2020, https://www.prindex.net/.

15. The MENA region is followed by Sub-Saharan Africa, which exhibits a 14-percentage point discrepancy between married women and married men about their fear of losing property in the case of a divorce or spousal death. Globally, the discrepancy is only 5 percentage points (see figure 11 in Prindex 2020).

16. Inheritance in Islam follows complex rules. For more details of Sunni and Shia interpretations of inheritance rules, see COHRE (2006); Ghamari-Tabrizi (2013); and Hanna (2020).

17. *Shari'a* law was applied to inheritance in Egypt until 2019. However, in November 2019, after strident legal activism by female Christian lawyer Huda Nasrallah, Cairo's Court of Appeal, in an unprecedented final judgment, confirmed the right of Coptic women to inherit equally. The judgment was based on Article 245 of the Orthodox personal status by-laws issued in 1938, which granted Coptic Christian women inheritance rights equal to those of men but was not enacted (Sidhom 2019).

18. WBL's Assets indicator measures women's ability to manage assets by ascertaining whether the law has the following provisions: (1) equal ownership rights to immovable property; (2) equal inheritance rights for sons and daughters; (3) equal inheritance rights for spouses; (4) equal administrative authority over assets during marriage; and (5) valuation of nonmonetary contributions. The other indicators are Going Places; Starting a Job; Getting Paid; Getting Married; Having Children; Running a Business; and Getting a Pension (World Bank 2020).

19. Only about 2 percent of women eligible to receive land mentioned that they legally renounced their share. Although these results are based on a small subsample (55) of women that faced a situation of inheritance, they are nevertheless indicative of the significant challenges faced by women in accessing land.

20. Palestinian women are six times less likely than men to use civil courts, and over a quarter of the Palestinian women polled said they would be prevented from resolving disputes in courts by social traditions and norms (UNDP 2017).

21. And to avoid land subdivision (*ifraz)* taxes.

22. The absence of land subdivision is very common in the MENA region. In Morocco, for example, 45 percent of private land (*mulk*) is not subdivided (FAO 2006). Everywhere, these patterns are exacerbated by the high costs of registering and subdividing property.

23. The United Nations' human settlement program, UN-Habitat, and the Office of the High Commissioner for Human Rights support property rights and the security of tenure under the Right to Adequate Housing Framework.

24. The Syrian conflict itself has led to a current situation in which 6.5 million internally displaced persons and 5.6 million registered refugees—probably many more unregistered—are being hosted in neighboring countries. Sectarian violence in Iraq against the Kurds and Shia populations between 2006 to 2008 led to the internal displacement of 2.7 million Iraqis, while 1.7 million took refuge abroad. Islamic State rule from January 2014 to October 2017 pushed 3 million refugees out of Mosul.

25. In accordance with recommendations in the Convention on the Elimination of All Forms of Discrimination Against Women (CEDAW), the Gaza office of UNRWA decided to include shared property titles for residents whose houses had been destroyed in 2014. The UNRWA Gaza Field Office Camp Rehabilitation promoted equal rehousing projects, and in 2015 a co-signing policy was introduced that requires heads of households and their spouse(s) to sign the undertaking together. The aim is to enable women and men to have equal property rights and access to housing (UNRWA 2017).

REFERENCES

Ababsa, M. 2017. "The Exclusion of Women from Property in Jordan: Inheritance Rights and Practices." *Hawwa* 15: 1–2, 107–28.

Al-Monitor. 2018. "Jordan Moves to Improve Lives of Gazan Refugees." December 11, 2018. https://www.al-monitor .com/originals/2018/12/jordan-gaza-refugees-palestinian-settlement.html.

Arab Barometer. 2020. "Women's Agency and Economic Mobility in MENA: Examining Patterns and Implications." February 13. https://www.arabbarometer.org/wp-content/uploads/Public_Opinion_Arab_Women_Economic _Conditions_Presentation_2020.pdf.

Benvenisti, E., and E. Zamir. 1995 "Private Claims to Property Rights in the Future Israeli-Palestinian Settlement." *American Journal of International Law* 89 (2): 295–340.

Campos, A., N. Warring, C. Brunelli, C. Doss, and C. Kieran. 2015. "Gender and Land Statistics: Recent Developments in FAO's Gender and Land Rights Database." Rome: Food and Agriculture Organization. http://www.fao .org/3/a-i4862e.pdf.

CAPMAS (Central Agency for Public Mobilization and Statistics). 2020. *Statistical Yearbook 2020.* Issue 111. Cairo: CAPMAS.

Christensen, I., B. Veillerette, and S. Andricopulos. 2007. "The Status of Rural Poverty in the Near East and North Africa." Food and Agriculture Organization and International Fund for Agricultural Development, Rome.

COHRE (Centre on Housing Rights and Evictions). 2006. "In Search of Equality: A Survey of Law and Practice Related to Women's Inheritance Rights in the Middle East and North Africa (MENA) Region." COHRE, Geneva.

ECWR (Egyptian Center for Women's Rights). 2017. "ECWR Welcomes the Amendment of the Inheritance Law." ECWR, Cairo. http://ecwronline.org/?p=7509.

FAO (Food and Agriculture Organization). 2006. "Rapport National du Royaume du Maroc." Conférence Internationale sur la Réforme Agraire et le Développement Rural (ICARRD), Porto Alegre, Brasil.

FAO (Food and Agriculture Organization)/IFAD (International Fund for Agricultural Development). 2007. *The Status of Rural Poverty in the Near East and North Africa.* Rome: FAO.

FAO (Food and Agriculture Organization), NRC (Norwegian Refugee Council), OCHA (United Nations Office for the Coordination of Humanitarian Affairs), UN-Habitat, and UNHCR (United Nations High Commissioner for Refugees). 2007. *Handbook on Housing and Property Restitution for Refugees and Displaced Persons: Implementing the "Pinheiro Principles."* https://www.un.org/ruleoflaw/blog/document/handbook-on-housing -and-property-restitution-for-refugees-and-displaced-persons-implementing-the-pinheiro-principles-2/.

Ghamari-Tabrizi, B. 2013. "Women's Rights, Shari'a Law, and the Secularization of Islam in Iran." *International Journal of Politics, Culture, and Society* 26: 237–53.

GIZ (Deutsche Gesellschaft für Internationale Zusammenarbeit). 2021. "Enquête des droits fonciers agricoles des femmes en Tunisie pour le projet Protection et réhabilitation de sols dégradées en Tunisie (ProSol)." Mission report prepared by BJKA Consulting, Ariana, Tunisia.

Hamilton, E., V. Mints, J. L. Acero Vergel, M. Ababsa, W. Tammaa, Y. Xiao, A. Molfetas-Lygkiaris, and J. R. Wille. 2018. *Jordan–Housing Sector Assessment–Housing Sector Review.* Washington, DC: World Bank.

Hanna, A. 2020. "The Iran Primer: Part 3: Iranian Laws on Women." United States Institute of Peace, Washington, DC. https://iranprimer.usip.org/blog/2020/dec/08/part-3-iranian-laws-women.

Haut Commissariat au Plan. 2019. "La femme marocaine en chiffres: évolution des caractéristiques démographiques et socio-professionnelles." http://www.hcp.ma.

IFAD (International Fund for Agricultural Development). 2013. "Enabling the Rural Poor to Overcome Poverty in Jordan." IFAD, Rome.

Jansen, W. 1993. "Creating Identities: Gender, Religion and Women's Property in Jordan." In *Who's Afraid of Femininity? Questions of Identity*, edited by M. Brugman, S. Heebing, and D. Long, 157–67. Amsterdam: Rodopi.

JNCW (Jordanian National Commission for Women). 2010. "Jordan's Fifth National Periodic Report to the CEDAW Committee—Summary." JNCW, Amman.

Jordan Times. 2018. "Gov't Adopts New Resolutions for Gazans with Temporary Passports." December 4, 2018. http://jordantimes.com/news/local/govt-adopts-new-resolutions-gazans-temporary-passports.

Lawry, S., C. Samii, R. Hall, A. Leopold, D. Hornby, and F. Mtero. 2017. "The Impact of Land Property Rights Interventions on Investment and Agricultural Productivity in Developing Countries: A Systematic Review." *Journal of Development Effectiveness* 9 (1): 61–81.

Meinzen-Dick, R., A. Quisumbing, C. Doss, and S. Theis. 2019. "Women's Land Rights as a Pathway to Poverty Reduction: Framework and Review of Available Evidence." *Agricultural Systems* 172: 72–82.

Ministry of Health and Population (Egypt), El-Zanaty and Associates (Egypt), and ICF International. 2015. *Egypt Demographic and Health Survey 2014.* Cairo: Ministry of Health and Population and ICF International. http://dhsprogram.com/pubs/pdf/FR302/FR302.pdf.

Naffa, L., F. Al Dabbas, A. Jabiri, and N. Al Emam. 2007. "Shadow NGO Report to CEDAW Committee Jordan: Evaluation of National Policy, Measures and Actual Facts on Violence Against Women." Karama Network of Jordan. http://www.el-karama.org/wp-content/uploads/2013/04/Final_JOR_NGOs_Shadow_Rept.pdf.

Najjar, D., B. Baruah, and A. El Garhi. 2020. "Gender and Asset Ownership in the Old and New Lands of Egypt." *Feminist Economics* 26 (3): 11943.

NRC (Norwegian Refugee Council). 2011. "The Shari'a Courts and Personal Status Laws in the Gaza Strip." NRC, Oslo.

NRC (Norwegian Refugee Council). 2017. "Displacement, HLP and Access to Civil Documentation in the South of the Syrian Arab Republic." NRC, Oslo.

OHCHR (Office of the High Commissioner for Human Rights). 2021. "Universal Periodic Review 2020: Palestinian Refugees Rights in Lebanon." UPR 37. United Nations Human Rights Council, Geneva.

Paglione, G. 2008. "Individual Property Restitution: From Deng to Pinheiro—and the Challenges Ahead." *International Journal of Refugee Law* 20 (3): 392–93.

Prettitore, P. 2013a. "Gender and Justice in Jordan: Women, Demand and Access." MENA Knowledge and Learning Quick Notes Series, No. 107, World Bank, Washington, DC.

Prettitore, P. 2013b. "Justice Sector Services and the Poor in Jordan: Determining Needs and Priorities." MENA Knowledge and Learning Quick Notes Series, No. 96, World Bank, Washington, DC.

Prindex. 2020. *Women's Perception of Tenure Security: Evidence from 140 Countries.* London: Prindex. https://www.prindex.net/reports/womens-perceptions-tenure-security-evidence-140-countries/.

Selod, H., and S. Soumahoro. Forthcoming. "The Arab Spring and the Politically 'Unlocked' Land." Background paper prepared for this report, World Bank, Washington, DC.

Sidhom, Y. 2019. "Court Ruling: Equal Inheritance for Men and Women." *Watani International.* http://en.wataninet.com/opinion/editorial/court-ruling-equal-inheritance-for-men-andwomen/29392/.

UNDP (United Nations Development Programme). 2017. *Public Perceptions of Palestinian Justice and Security Institutions in 2015.* 3rd ed. Programme of Assistance to the Palestinian People, UNDP, Jerusalem. https://www.ps.undp.org/content/papp/en/home/library/democratic_governance/public-perceptions-of-palestinian-justice-and-security-instituti0.html.

UNDP (United Nations Development Programme). 2018. *2018 Statistical Update: Human Development Indices and Indicators.* New York: UNDP. https://hdr.undp.org/en/content/human-development-indices-indicators-2018-statistical-update.

UNESC (United Nations Economic and Social Council). 2005. *Housing and Property Restitution in the Context of the Return of Refugees and Internally Displaced Persons: Final Report of the Special Rapporteur, Paulo Sérgio Pinheiro.* https://www.unhcr.org/uk/protection/idps/50f94d849/principles-housing-property-restitution-refugees-displaced-persons-pinheiro.html.

Unruh, J. D. 2016. "Mass Claims in Land and Property Following the Arab Spring: Lessons from Yemen." *Stability: International Journal of Security and Development* 5 (1): 6.

UNRWA (United Nations Relief and Works Agency for Palestine Refugees in the Near East). 2017. *Integrating Gender, Improving Services, Impacting Lives: Gender Equality Strategy 2016–2021.* Amman, Jordan, and Gaza, Palestinian Authority: UNRWA.

USAID (US Agency for International Development). 2016. "Fact Sheet: Land Tenure and Women's Empowerment." https://www.land-links.org/wp-content/uploads/2016/11/USAID_Land_Tenure_Women_Land_Rights_Fact_Sheet.pdf.

Vignal, L. 2019. "Locating Dispossession and HLP Rights in the War in Syria." In *Reclaiming Home: The Struggle for Socially Just Housing, Land and Property Rights in Syria, Iraq and Libya,* edited by H. Baumann, 18–31. Washington, DC: Friedrich-Ebert-Stiftung Foundation.

WCLAC (Women's Centre for Legal Aid and Counselling). 2014. "Palestinian Women and Inheritance." http://www.wclac.org/english/userfiles/Translated%20Inheritance%20Study%20English.pdf.

World Bank. 2011. *World Development Report 2012: Gender Equality and Development.* Washington, DC: World Bank.

World Bank. 2013. *Opening Doors: Gender Equality and Development in the Middle East and North Africa.* Washington, DC: World Bank.

World Bank. 2019. "Gender and Land Survey: West Bank and Gaza." Unpublished report. World Bank, Washington, DC.

World Bank. 2020. *Women, Business and the Law 2020.* Washington, DC: World Bank.

World Bank. Forthcoming. *Land, Conflict, and Inclusion.* Washington, DC: World Bank.

Yahya, M. 2018. *The Politics of Dispossession.* Beirut: The Malcolm H. Kerr Carnegie Middle East Center.

CHAPTER 4

Market Distortions and Land Use Inefficiencies in the MENA Region

INTRODUCTION

The constraints on the land sector in terms of use and access described in the previous chapter are likely to have stark implications for Middle East and North Africa (MENA) economies. This chapter examines the channels through which distortions could emerge and their economic implications. It also presents empirical analyses of two examples of policies that address land issues in terms of both efficiency of use and access: industrial zones in the Arab Republic of Egypt and taxation of vacant land in Saudi Arabia.

EXPANDED CONCEPTUAL FRAMEWORK

The key notion underpinning the study described in this report is that because of physical constraints, institutional constraints, and to some extent ill-inspired or ill-conceived policies, land is inefficiently used (or misallocated) in MENA countries. The conceptual framework described in this section—an expansion of the conceptual framework laid out in figure I.1 in the introduction of this report—reveals the channels through which land use inefficiencies in MENA may emerge and pinpoints their possible economic, environmental, and social impacts.

Figure 4.1 details the main paths through which land scarcity and institutional constraints (and their interactions with policies) can introduce distortions in the economy and lead to suboptimal utilization of land with its economic, environmental, and social costs. As shown in figure 4.1, such distortions may involve nonmarket prices of land and of other factors, high land transaction costs, land tenure insecurity, or credit constraints. For example, institutional

Figure 4.1 Conceptual framework for land misallocation, MENA

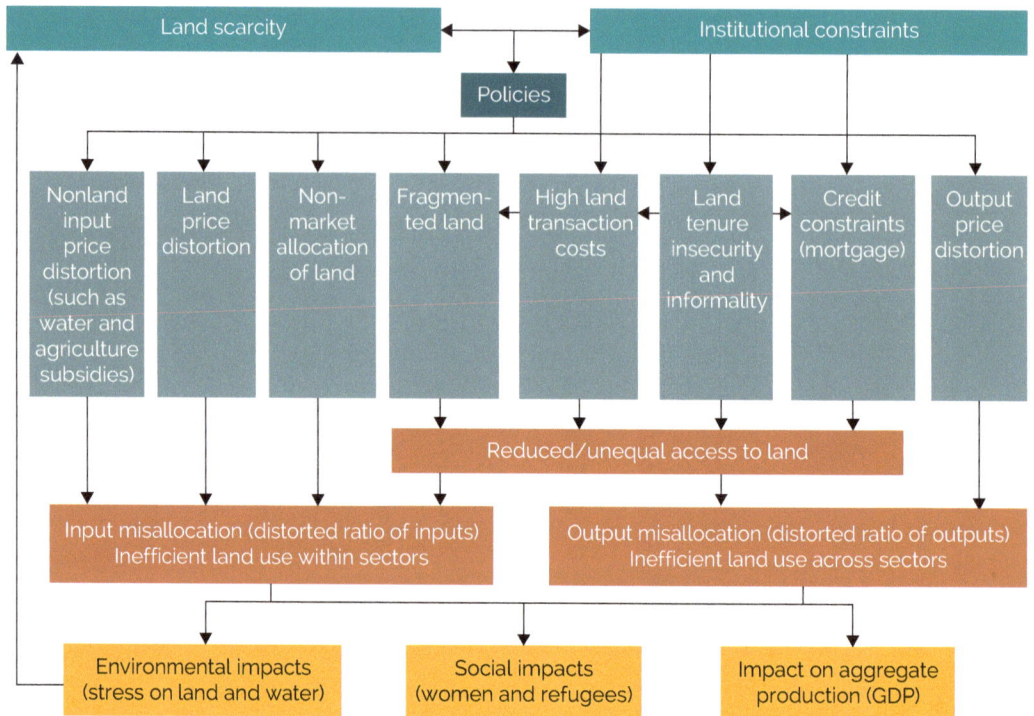

Land scarcity						Institutional constraints	

Policies

Nonland input price distortion (such as water and agriculture subsidies)	Land price distortion	Non-market allocation of land	Fragmented land	High land transaction costs	Land tenure insecurity and informality	Credit constraints (mortgage)	Output price distortion

Reduced/unequal access to land

Input misallocation (distorted ratio of inputs) Inefficient land use within sectors	Output misallocation (distorted ratio of outputs) Inefficient land use across sectors

Environmental impacts (stress on land and water)	Social impacts (women and refugees)	Impact on aggregate production (GDP)

Source: World Bank.

constraints that reduce access to credit can lead to underinvestment in land, low agricultural production, and limited job creation. By contrast, subsidies for agricultural inputs may increase the use of land for agriculture, potentially serving the policy objectives of improving food sovereignty and creating jobs. Such outcomes may, however, be achieved at the cost of water pollution and depletion, land degradation, and a reduced capacity to respond to climate challenges in the future.

Land misallocation can affect production, environmental sustainability, and inclusion. Misallocation can affect production when land is disproportionately used by nonproductive firms and sectors at the expense of more productive firms and sectors. In economic terms, this use leads to lower output than would have been possible because of the suboptimal use of the land—that is, output is produced inefficiently; investment is suboptimal in the face of distorted incentives; or inefficient firms and sectors are artificially maintained afloat.[1] In broader terms, land misallocation can be understood in terms of sustainability when environmental externalities call into question the desirability of current land uses. One of the main consequences of the misuse of the land in the MENA region—whether residential, industrial, or agricultural—is water stress and water depletion. Finally, land misallocation can also have social consequences when limited access of vulnerable groups and women to land constrains their economic opportunities and exacerbates poverty.

Land misallocation can result from the physical constraints and institutional challenges faced by MENA economies, as well as their policy choices. The location of human activities in areas prone to flooding, for example, can be viewed as misuse of land. In many instances, land misallocation can also stem from institutional or regulatory constraints. Examples include laws and regulations (such as floor area ratio ceilings in Tunisia or minimum lot size requirements in Jordan) that produce sprawl in cities, unclear property rights that deter investments in land, or processes of land allocation outside markets, combined with high transaction costs, that result in land not being used most efficiently. Land misallocation can also stem from economic policies, such as subsidies for agriculture and water, leading to use of an excessive amount of land for agriculture.

Land fragmentation could also be a form of misallocation if associated with lower productivity (which is especially likely if returns to scale in agriculture make larger farms more productive). Although state-of-the-art analyses of farmland misallocation are still lacking for the region, there is reason to believe that such misallocation could be problematic, especially in the Maghreb countries and Egypt, which have the largest proportion of small farms in the region (see figure 4A.1 in annex 4A, which shows the distribution of agricultural land in 11 MENA countries). Unfortunately, the issue of land misallocation, an emerging topic in economics, has barely been studied in the context of MENA countries.

LAND DISTORTIONS IN MENA ECONOMIES

In light of the framework just presented, this section discusses in more detail a few examples of the distortions affecting land or resulting from weaknesses in land administration and management in the MENA region.

Credit and mortgage markets are limited in the region likely due largely to the low levels of land registration. This limitation is particularly acute in Algeria, Egypt, and Jordan. As shown in figure 4.2, in these countries the size of mortgage markets as a percentage of GDP is less than 2 percent, compared with 22 percent in Kuwait and 27 percent in Israel.[2] Important binding constraints that prevent development of these markets are the low levels of land registration and the impossibility of using nonregistered land as collateral, which restricts both firms' and households' access to funds for investment. Figure 4.3 illustrates this point by plotting housing loan penetration (defined as the percentage of adults with an outstanding loan to purchase a home) against the Geographic Coverage index from Doing Business (see box 2.4 in chapter 2). The figure shows a positive association between the coverage of land registries and use of housing finance. The foregone opportunities from reduced access to funding because of lack of registration are likely to be very large. For example, a 2018 study in the West Bank reveals that the potential collateral value of unregistered land would range from US$7 billion to as much as US$35 billion (for a GDP of US$16 billion at the time).

Access to international financial markets and capital is also restricted because of the difficulties foreigners may face with accessing or owning land in MENA countries. In Morocco, the complexities of the legal framework for access to certain lands (such as customary lands) restrict foreigners from investing in certain economic sectors such as agriculture. In the Republic of Yemen, prior to its post–Arab Spring political turmoil and conflict, inconsistencies in the country's land governance and legal framework also constrained foreign access to land and investment. In addition to overlapping Islamic and customary forms of tenure, one law in the Yemeni legal framework allowed up to 100 percent ownership interest of land for foreigners, while another law allowed only up to 49 percent of ownership interest, with neither law negating the other (USAID 2010). The inconsistency in the laws, combined with confusion over what land tenure system—the Republic of Yemen's official legal framework, Islamic law, or customary law—was the source of legitimacy for enforcing property rights in different parts of the country, acted as a major barrier to foreign access to land and investment.

Figure 4.2 Mortgage loans, MENA, 2015

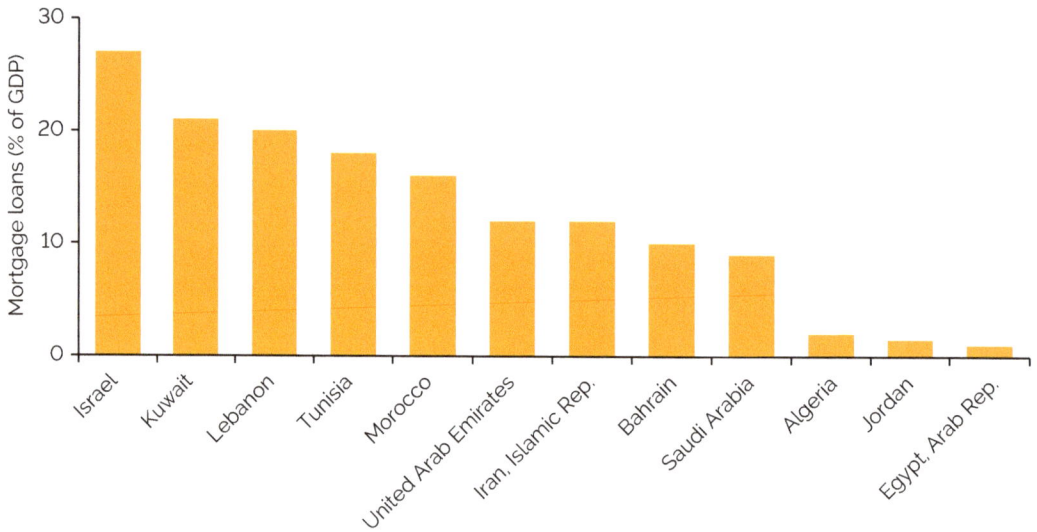

Sources: Central banks; Wharton School of the University of Pennsylvania, International Finance Corporation, and Entrepreneurial Development Bank (FMO), Housing Finance Information Network (HOFINET) (dashboard), http://www.hofinet.org.
Note: Data for the United Arab Emirates and Algeria are for earlier years.

Figure 4.3 Housing loan penetration and registration coverage, MENA and rest of the world

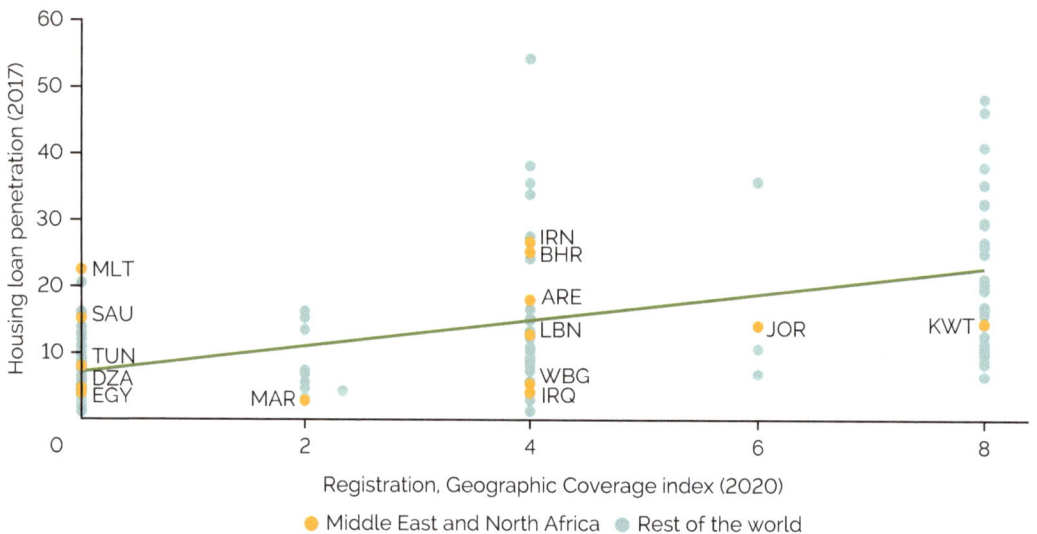

Sources: World Bank, Global Findex Database 2017 (dashboard), https://globalfindex.worldbank.org/; World Bank, Doing Business 2004–2020 (database), https://archive.doingbusiness.org/en/doingbusiness.
Note: See figure 1.4 for country codes.

Vacant land (in the Gulf countries) or vacant residential units (in Egypt, Jordan, and Lebanon) in prime urban areas are sources of inefficient land use in MENA cities. Land could be vacant for multiple reasons, ranging from barriers to formally developing the land to the speculative behaviors of some landholders, who find it preferable to keep the property idle. Vacant residential units are a more surprising phenomenon, but they are nevertheless very common in some cities. In Egypt, vacant residential units are found in the new cities built by the government in the desert away from the congested old cities. These vacant units primarily serve to attract the savings of the upper and middle classes (in the absence of other savings opportunities and in anticipation that these locations will become more attractive), but jobs have not massively relocated to the new cities and remain largely located in old cities. In Jordan, it is estimated that in Amman almost one in four units is vacant. In Lebanon, 23 percent of housing units developed between 1996 and 2018 are unoccupied, and one out of two apartments in the high-end market is vacant. The vacancy of residential units may likely have multiple causes. In Lebanon, the exemptions of vacant units from property tax incentivizes owners to keep their properties empty, expecting capital gains from their investments rather than rental income.[3]

Barriers to land registration and the costs to access formal housing contribute to informal tenure and slums. Slums are widespread in the MENA region. It is estimated that over 24 percent of the urban population in the region live in slums, and the proportion of the urban population residing informally—a larger category than slums—is likely significantly greater.[4] Although the likely causes of informal housing vary, an important factor is the land administration and governance challenges that prevent the delivery and update of property rights following land transactions. Figure 4.4 plots the share of the urban slums against the cost of property registration (as a percentage of property value). The clear positive association suggests that barriers to registration (including financial barriers) are an important potential driver of informal housing.

Figure 4.4 Slums and cost of property registration, MENA and rest of the world

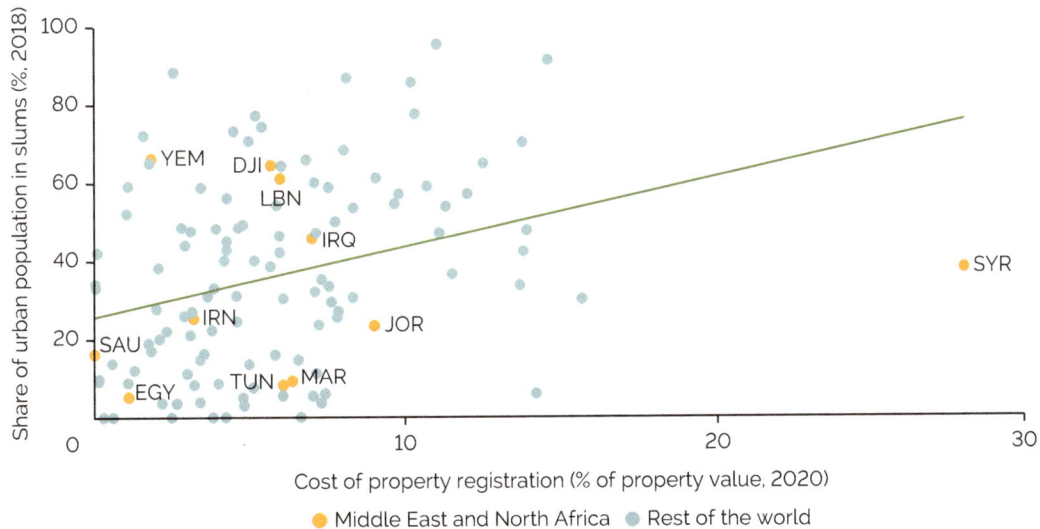

Sources: United Nations Human Settlements Programme (UN-Habitat), available at World Bank, Data, https://data.worldbank.org /indicator/en.pop.slum.ur.zs; World Bank, Doing Business 2004–2020 (database), https://archive.doingbusiness.org/en/doingbusiness. Note: See figure 1.4 for country codes.

Urban planning weaknesses and failures of central and local governments to make land available for formal development also explain the proliferation of slums. Because of restrictions on the formal supply of land, the production of formal housing remains limited, resulting in high housing prices that are unaffordable to the poor or even to the middle classes. In Iraq, for example, it is estimated that during the last decade the production of formal housing only covered 10–14 percent of annual housing needs. In all countries, low-income groups are struggling to afford formal land and housing. Social housing is high on the agenda in MENA countries, but existing programs are often limited in scope.

Although informal markets perform a social function by housing the poor, they are also characterized by tenure insecurity and disputes, high-cost services, poor-quality structures, and negative externalities on the environment. Informal housing removes significant portions of cities from the formal land market and from the fiscal base. Expansion of informal housing at the periphery of cities also contributes to the degradation of agricultural land and informal conversion of land uses outside urban plans.

POLICIES

Industrial Zones (Egypt)

The creation of industrial zones in the MENA region has facilitated firms' access to land. In the region, as in many other regions of the world, there is a push toward policy interventions to create geographic zones that will attract investments and create jobs—at times with the help of fiscal incentives. In the developing world, in addition to facilitating the concentration of activities in clusters, an important underlying motivation for the establishment of such zones is to allow pooling and servicing the land required for productive manufacturing activities.[5] Egypt is probably the country in the MENA region with the largest program of industrial zones. However, since their launch in the 1970s Egypt has had mixed success because some of its industrial zones have had difficulty attracting investments (World Bank 2006, 2009). Using a georeferenced database of Egyptian industrial zones generated for this report by Corsi et al. (forthcoming), figure 4.5 shows that in Egypt industrial zones are increasingly being created farther from cities. Analysis of the same data shows that a dozen such zones of those created since the mid-1990s are located more than 100 kilometers (and sometimes more than 200 kilometers) from cities of 200,000 residents or more. This finding likely illustrates a tendency of the Egyptian government to use for industrial zones desert land that it owns and can more easily convert to industrial use, thereby avoiding lengthy conflicts about land ownership and use. It also illustrates an increasing tendency to set up industrial zones in more remote areas, possibly with the goal of creating jobs in lagging regions after giving priority to the creation of industrial zones in more populated areas over the previous decades.

However, most industrial zones are only partially occupied, with the utilization rate (percentage of land in a zone occupied by firms) greater for industrial zones closer to cities. As shown in figure 4.6, industrial zones located less than 50 kilometers from a city with more than 200,000 residents have a utilization rate of about 56 percent, whereas the utilization rate is less than 10 percent for industrial zones located more than 150 kilometers from a city with more than 200,000 inhabitants. Figure 4.6 also illustrates that much time is needed for industrial zones to attract firms, and that enterprise zones are only rarely fully occupied. The occupation rate for industrial zones established less than 10 years ago is on average about 22 percent, whereas it is about 86 percent for industrial zones created more than 30 years ago. In fact, even longtime industrial zones may only partially fill up when located far from cities. For example, an industrial zone shown in figure 4.6 was created 25 years ago about 175 kilometers from a city of more than 200,000 residents, but it is only half-occupied to date. These observations are confirmed by the background analysis for this report, which reveals that location and date of establishment are statistical predictors of an industrial zone's utilization rate. Perhaps the main lesson from this assessment is that labor pooling—which such clusters of firms require—is simply not feasible when these zones are spatially disconnected from cities and markets.

Figure 4.5 Egyptian industrial zones, by distance from cities with more than 200,000 residents and year of creation, 1927–2020

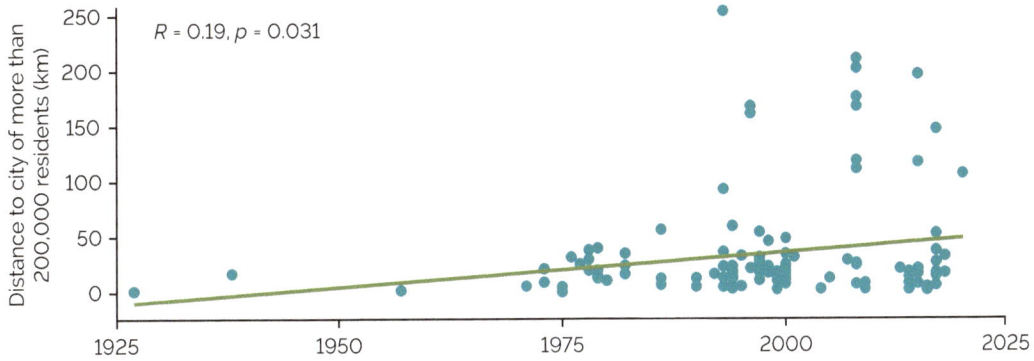

Source: Authors' calculations, based on Corsi et al. (forthcoming).
Note: The graph plots the distance of industrial zones to the nearest city of over 200,000 residents against their year of establishment. km = kilometers.

Figure 4.6 Utilization rate of Egyptian industrial zones, by distance from cities with more than 200,000 residents and length of time since creation

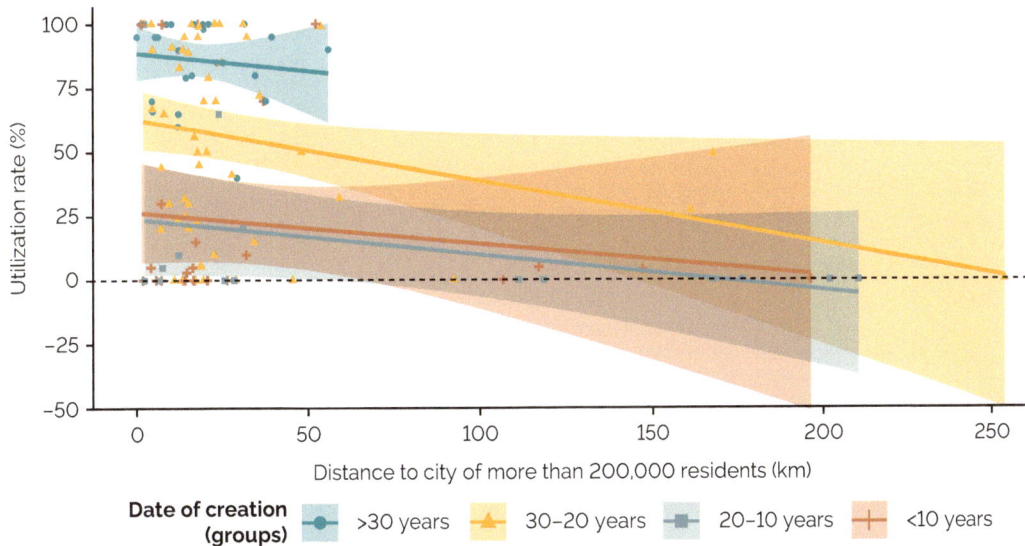

Source: Authors' calculations, based on Corsi et al. (forthcoming).
Note: The graph plots the utilization rate of industrial zones defined as the share of land in an industrial zone that is occupied by firms against distance to the nearest city of more than 200,000 residents. Industrial zones are grouped according to the number of years since their creation. A fit and 95 percent confidence interval are represented for each group. km = kilometers.

Vacant Land Tax (Saudi Arabia)

The introduction of a vacant land tax in 2016 in Saudi Arabia was aimed at increasing the supply of plots in large cities, improving the affordability of housing, and discouraging monopolistic behaviors in urban areas. The prevalence of vacant land (so-called white land) in Saudi cities has long been debated, especially because of the rising demand for urban land, driven in part by a steadily increasing urban population (1.7 percent a year since 2000). In 2010, an influential study on housing in Riyadh estimated that 77 percent of the city's land stood idle, prompting an intense debate in the popular press and calls for government action. Saudi Arabia's response was announced in 2013 with a draft bill of the consultative assembly (Shura Council) proposing a vacant land tax, which became effective in 2016 and was applied to four major cities (Riyadh, Jeddah, Dammam, and Khobar). The 2.5 percent tax was levied on idle land plots of 10,000 square meters. Toward the end of 2020, a second phase of the policy was announced, broadening the criteria for taxation eligibility. It now covered idle land of 10,000 square meters or more irrespective of the number of owners of the plot, as well as land plots owned by the same owner that when consolidated totaled 10,000 square meters or more.[6]

The total area of land sales and the number of transactions increased significantly in targeted cities during the preparation phase of the white land tax policy in both commercial and residential areas. Figure 4.7 plots the total amount of commercially zoned land (panel a) and residentially zoned land (panel b) that were sold each month in the four targeted cities after the policy was announced in 2013 (vertical dashed line). As expected, the figure clearly shows that a large amount of land was sold prior to policy implementation in 2016 (vertical solid line), which did not occur in nontargeted cities (not shown in the figure). For more details, see the background research undertaken for this report that investigated the causal effect of the policy on land sales over time in comparing monthly land sales in targeted and nontargeted cities over time (Alkhowaiter, Selod, and Soumahoro, forthcoming). Preliminary results from the study confirm a large causal effect in anticipation of taxation (as suggested by figure 4.7) and an additional increase in land sales following the announcement and implementation of broader taxation criteria at the end of 2020 (phase two). The phase two effect is mostly for small plots, suggesting that large landowners subdivided their plots before selling them on the market.

Figure 4.7 **Total area sold before and after implementation of vacant land tax in four cities, Saudi Arabia**

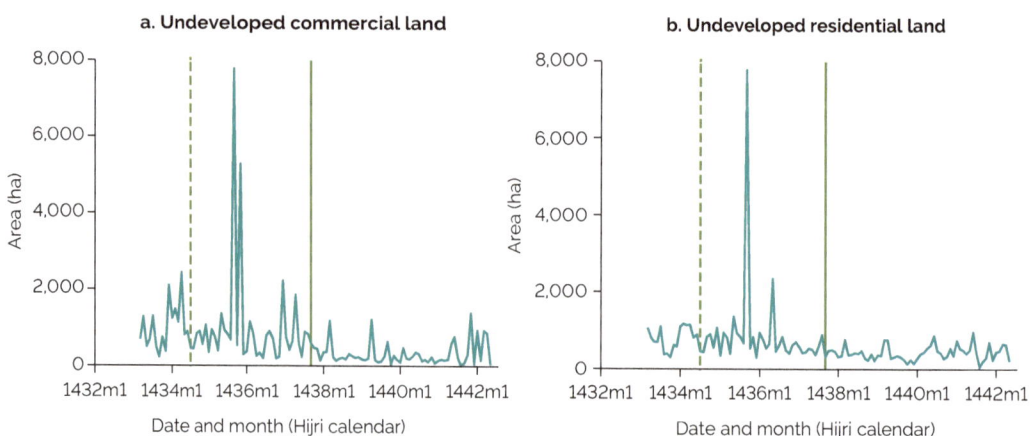

Source: Authors' calculations, based on data provided by Saudi Arabia Ministry of Justice.
Note: The vertical dashed line indicates when the taxation policy was introduced in 2013 (Hijri 1434). The vertical solid line indicates when the taxation policy was implemented in 2016 (Hijri 1437). ha = hectares.

ANNEX 4A: THE DISTRIBUTION OF FARMLAND

Figure 4A.1 presents Lorenz curves for the distribution of "landholdings" (farms) and land using data from the Food and Agriculture Organization's World Programme for the Census of Agriculture (FAO 2020). It shows the cumulative percentage of land utilized by the cumulative percentage of farms. Gulf Cooperation Council (GCC) countries (especially Saudi Arabia and Qatar) have Lorenz curves that are the closest to the bottom-right corner, indicating the prominence of very large farms (as in the GCC countries), which occupy a very large fraction of the land. Conversely, Algeria, Egypt, Morocco, and Tunisia have Lorenz curves farther from the bottom-right corner, indicating the presence of numerous small farms that occupy a large fraction of the land in total.

Figure 4A.1 Distribution of agricultural land, MENA, various years

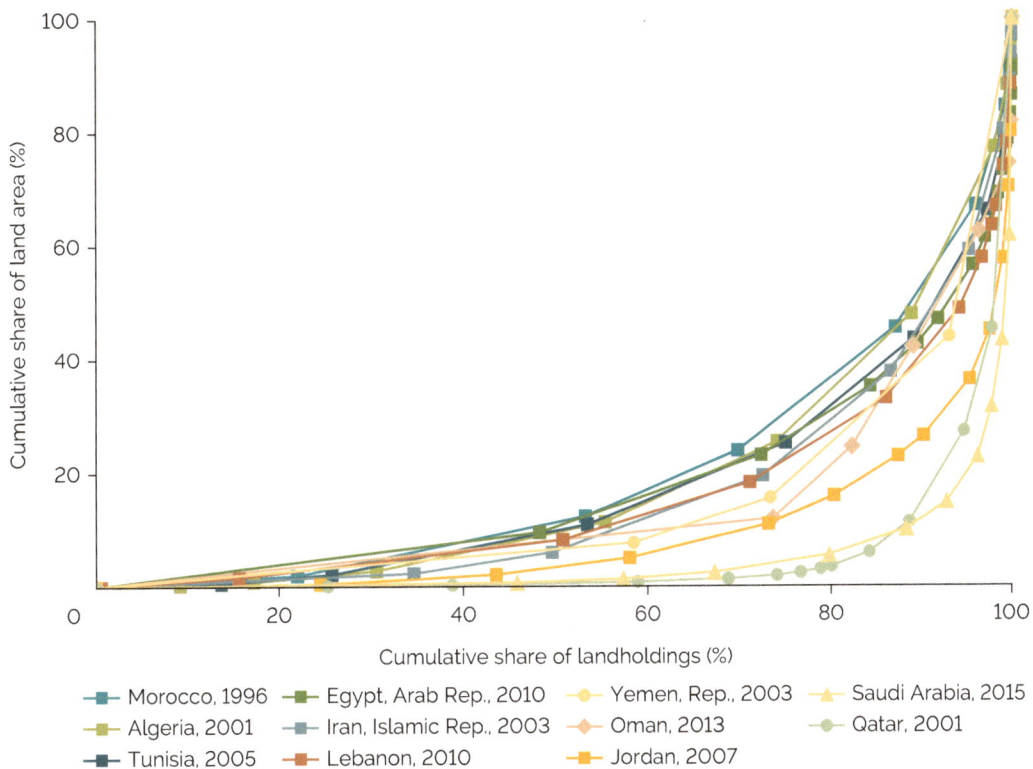

Source: FAO 2020.
Note: The graph reflects the most recent data available.

NOTES

1. *Land misallocation* can be defined as a situation in which there is not an optimal allocation of land. In an economy with no misallocation, marginal products of inputs are equalized across production entities, such as firms or farms, so that there is no increase in output if inputs are reallocated across the production entities. Any allocation that differs from efficient allocation, even if more factors are allocated to more productive entities, will generate lower aggregate output. The cost of misallocation is typically measured as the loss in aggregate total factor productivity (TFP) or output, compared with a situation in which marginal products would be equalized. For seminal papers on misallocation, see Olley and Pakes (1996) and Hsieh and Klenow (2009).

For papers on land misallocation in various contexts, see Adamopoulos and Restuccia (2019); Ali, Deininger, and Ronchi (2019); Besley and Burgess (2000); Duranton et al. (2015); Glaeser (2014); Glaeser and Ward (2009); Oldenburg (1990); Restuccia and Santaeulalia-Llopis (2017); and Sood (2019). For a short synthesis, see Restuccia (2020).

2. Typically, this indicator is much higher in member countries of the Organisation for Economic Co-operation and Development (OECD). For example, it reaches 46 percent in France, 60 percent in the United States, and 64 percent in the United Kingdom.

3. Of course, these figures could also hide some level of misreporting to avoid taxation.

4. Figures on the share of formal dwellings are hard to come by. In 1996, it was estimated that only 27 percent of dwellings could be considered formal in Cairo, and recent estimates indicate a figure closer to 10 percent.

5. In advanced countries, where fewer market failures stem from difficult access to land, there is a debate about whether industrial zones are successful. Some economists point out that agglomeration can be achieved more efficiently when left to firms rather than the decisions of public authorities. For a review of place-based policies, including special economic zones, see Duranton and Venables (2018).

6. These broader criteria reduced the scope for avoidance strategies (such as partitioning plots among family members).

REFERENCES

Adamopoulos, T., and D. Restuccia. 2019. "Land Reform and Productivity: A Quantitative Analysis with Micro Data." NBER Working Paper w25780, National Bureau of Economic Research, Cambridge, MA.

Ali, D. A., K. Deininger, and L. Ronchi. 2019. "Costs and Benefits of Land Fragmentation: Evidence from Rwanda." *World Bank Economic Review* 33 (3): 750–71.

Alkhowaiter, M., H. Selod, and S. Soumahoro. Forthcoming. "Unlocking Idle Land." Background paper prepared for this report, World Bank, Washington, DC.

Besley, T., and R. Burgess. 2000. "Land Reform, Poverty Reduction, and Growth: Evidence from India." *Quarterly Journal of Economics* 115 (2): 389–430.

Corsi, A., M. Elgarf, M. Nada, H. Park, and H. Selod. Forthcoming. "Industrial Zones in Egypt—An Assessment." Background paper prepared for this report, World Bank, Washington, DC.

Duranton, G., E. Ghani, A. Grover, and W. Kerr. 2015. "The Misallocation of Land and Other Factors of Production in India." Policy Research Working Paper 7221, World Bank, Washington, DC.

Duranton, G., and A. J. Venables. 2018. "Place-Based Policies for Development." Policy Research Working Paper 8410, World Bank, Washington, DC.

FAO (Food and Agriculture Organization). 2020. "World Programme for the Census of Agriculture." FAO, Rome. https://www.fao.org/world-census-agriculture/en/.

Glaeser, E. L. 2014. "Land Use Restrictions and Other Barriers to Growth." Cato Institute, Washington, DC.

Glaeser, E. L., and B. A. Ward. 2009. "The Causes and Consequences of Land Use Regulation: Evidence from Greater Boston." *Journal of Urban Economics* 65 (3): 265–78.

Hsieh, C. T., and P. J. Klenow. 2009. "Misallocation and Manufacturing TFP in China and India." *Quarterly Journal of Economics* 124 (4): 1403–48.

Oldenburg, P. 1990. "Land Consolidation as Land Reform, in India." *World Development* 18 (2): 183–95.

Olley, G. S., and A. Pakes. 1996. "The Dynamics of Productivity in the Telecommunications Equipment Industry." *Econometrica: Journal of the Econometric Society* 64 (6): 1263–97.

Restuccia, D. 2020. "The Impact of Land Institutions and Misallocation on Agricultural Productivity." *The Reporter*, No. 1, March. National Bureau of Economic Research, Cambridge, MA. https://www.nber.org /reporter/2020number1/impact-land-institutions-and-misallocation-agricultural-productivity.

Restuccia, D., and R. Santaeulalia-Llopis. 2017. "Land Misallocation and Productivity." NBER Working Paper 23128, National Bureau of Economic Research, Cambridge, MA.

Sood, A. 2019. "Land Market Frictions and Manufacturing in India." Working paper, University of Michigan, Ann Arbor.

USAID (US Agency for International Development). 2010. "USAID Country Profile—Property Rights and Resource Governance—Yemen." https://www.land-links.org/wp-content/uploads/2016/09/USAID_Land_Tenure_Yemen _Profile-1.pdf.

World Bank. 2006. *Arab Republic of Egypt. Public Land Management Strategy. Volume II: Background Notes on Access to Public Land by Investment Sector: Industry, Tourism, Agriculture and Real Estate Development.* Washington, DC: World Bank.

World Bank. 2009. "Reassessing the State's Role in Industrial Land Markets." In *From Privilege to Competition: Unlocking Private-Led Growth in the Middle East and North Africa.* Washington, DC: World Bank.

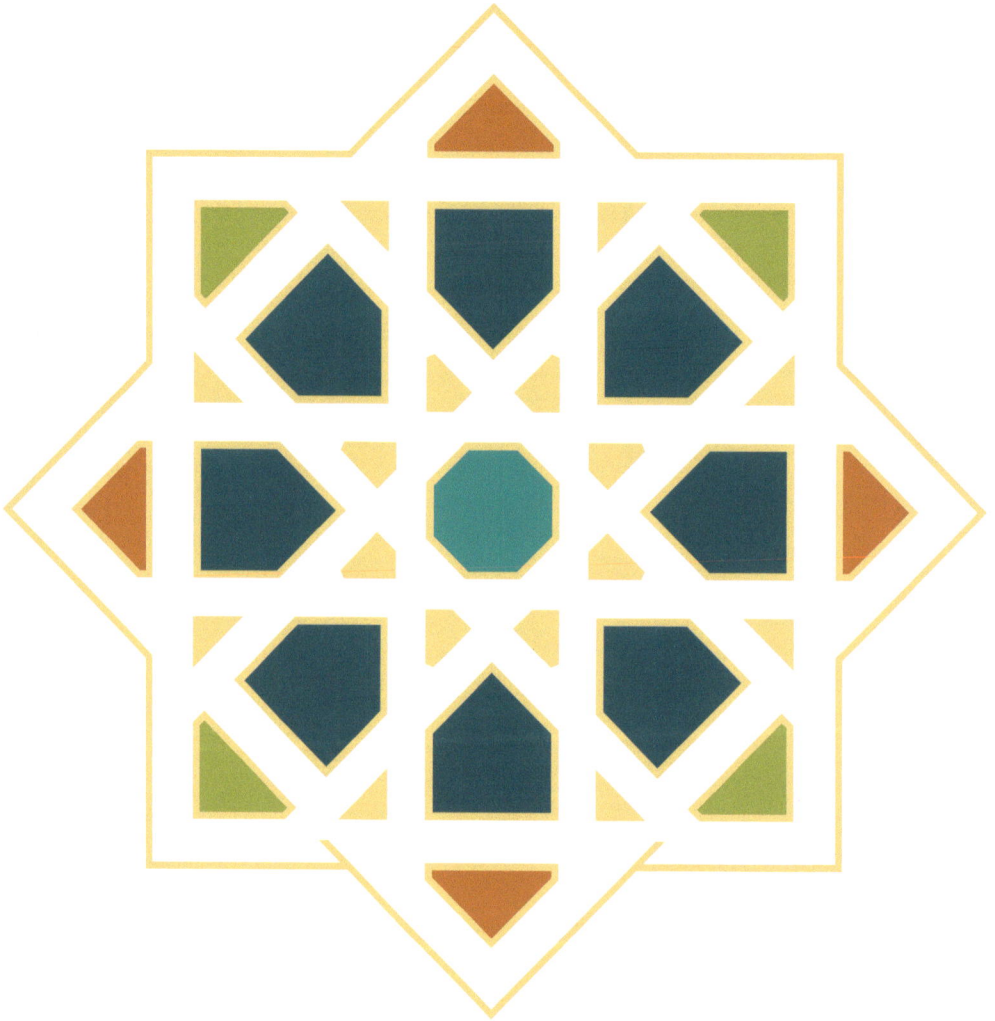

CHAPTER 5

Land Policy Challenges and Options in the MENA Region

INTRODUCTION

The picture that emerges from this report is one of a looming regional crisis stemming from increasingly scarce land, issues of food sovereignty and security, fast population growth, conflict, and civil society tensions. As shown in the previous chapters, these issues and the worsening trends underlying them are exacerbated by weak governance of land, including gender disparities in access to land. Not all countries in the region, however, face issues having the same severity. The chapter thus begins by proposing a taxonomy that identifies groups of countries according to the extent of these challenges. For the priority policy areas identified in the report and in light of the country taxonomy, the chapter then discusses policies that have been applied by countries in the Middle East and North Africa (MENA) and policy options to be considered moving forward in both the short and longer term.

A COUNTRY TAXONOMY OF CHALLENGES

A statistical analysis revealed that countries in the MENA region can be grouped by the severity of the land governance and land scarcity challenges they face, with implications for their policy choices (annex 5A). The groupings are based on two key aggregate dimensions or components: (1) weakness of governance and demographic pressure and (2) land availability. The first component mainly captures how countries are faring with respect to land governance, as measured by the Doing Business Quality of Land Administration index; the gender gap, as measured by the Gender Inequality Index of the United Nations Development

Programme (UNDP); and the challenge of future population growth, as measured by the United Nations' predicted percentage increase in population by 2050.[1] The second component mainly captures agricultural land availability, as measured by estimates of cropland per capita and remaining uncultivated land that could be used for rainfed agriculture.[2]

Country scores along these two aggregate dimensions are shown in figure 5.1. The striking result is that the typology groups countries by geographic proximity. The three main groups are as follows:

- *Bottom-left quadrant.* This quadrant includes countries that face severe land scarcity and a limited ability to respond to the predicted increased demand for land from future population growth. Yet they are the wealthier countries and tend to have relatively good land governance and relatively less gender inequality. This group consists of the six Gulf Cooperation Council (GCC) countries and Malta. Although governance efforts will still need to be pursued (especially on transparency and public land management), these countries will have to draw up a road map (based on robust social, economic, and environmental analyses) for addressing strategic trade-offs for the use of their land.
- *Upper-right quadrant.* Conversely, this quadrant contains countries with relatively more available land (although still scarce), but with weak land governance and strong gender inequality. This quadrant contains the Maghreb countries (with Tunisia slightly outside the border of this quadrant because of its relatively lower-than-expected population growth) as well as the cluster of countries composed of Iraq, the Islamic Republic of Iran, and the Syrian Arab Republic. Lebanon could also be added to this group because of its weak governance scores and the fact that it is outside the quadrant due to its expected declining population (which stands in stark contrast with that of the rest of the region). Although these countries tend to face less dramatic issues of land scarcity, they will still need to respond to the demand for land from population growth and to make significant progress on land governance.
- *Bottom-right quadrant.* The countries in this group have weak land governance, high gender inequality, very high expected population growth, and severe land scarcity. This quadrant contains countries in the Red Sea region (the Arab Republic of Egypt, Djibouti, and the Republic of Yemen) as well as the West Bank and Gaza. It is in these economies that the looming crisis of land scarcity is most evident and most challenging because, in contrast with the GCC countries, their weak land governance precludes immediate efficient responses. Jordan, despite its progress on governance, is in the same quadrant because of its high gender inequality, high expected population growth, and relative land scarcity. For the countries in this quadrant, improving land governance while addressing land trade-offs will be crucial. However, the land scarcity challenge cannot be addressed effectively if land governance is not improved (for example, knowledge of the land inventory is a prerequisite for making informed decisions about land use and allocations). However, sweeping reforms, although needed, may be impractical, and gradual approaches are likely more feasible.

The sections that follow discuss in detail how reforms in the land sector can help the country groups address the challenges discussed in this report, identifying reforms that are feasible in the short term and those that will require a strong political commitment and can only be achieved in the longer term.

Figure 5.1 MENA country taxonomy according to land availability, weak land governance, and demographic pressure

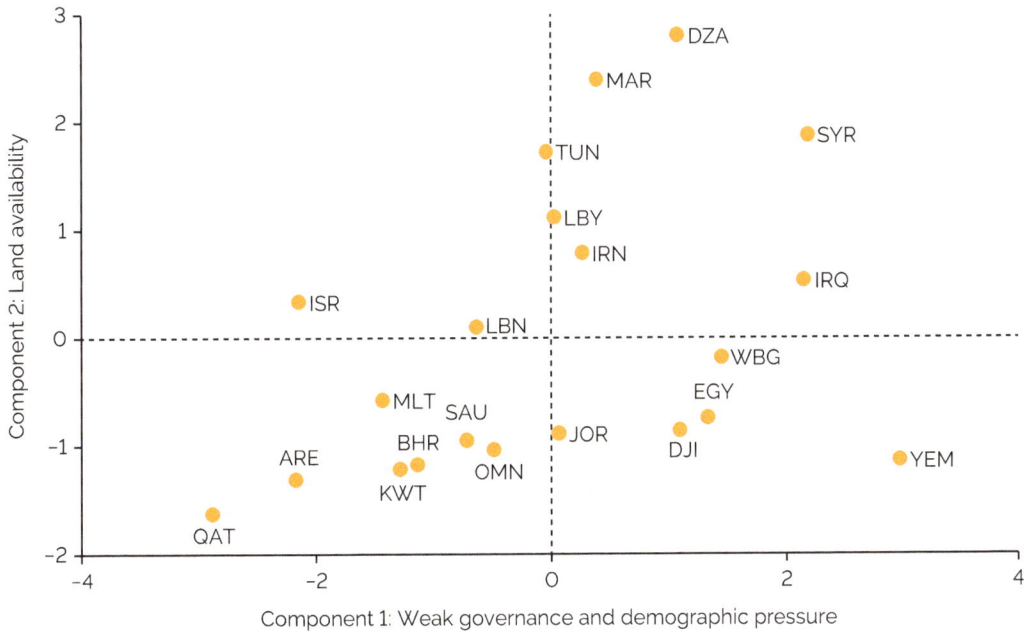

Source: World Bank.
Note: This country taxonomy is the outcome of the principal component analysis presented in annex 5A. The horizontal axis associates positive values with countries with weak governance and strong demographic pressure. The vertical axis associates positive values with countries where land is relatively more available. Rotation: orthogonal varimax. See figure 1.4 for country codes.

IMPROVING LAND ADMINISTRATION AND TENURE

Making informed decisions and improving land allocation and land use will depend on modernization of land administration. Assessments of the gaps and constraints in technical, financial, and operational capacity will help each country determine the extent of needed reforms and what will be a feasible road map. Policies aimed at the modernization of land administration have been implemented in the Gulf countries and are being considered or formulated in Egypt, Jordan, Lebanon, Morocco, Tunisia, and the West Bank and Gaza.

Jordan has made considerable progress since 1995 in completing its registration of most private land,[3] digitizing all records, providing online services, and consolidating mandates for both private and state land management. Despite these successes, however, Jordan still faces challenges, particularly the poor definition and documentation of state land (which is 80 percent of all land) and its management and the lack of clarity on customary rights, resulting in large-scale tenure insecurity (USAID 2018).

An example of a recently renewed effort toward modernization is the "Road Map for Reforming the Palestinian Land Sector" adopted by the Palestinian Authority in 2017.[4] What is notable about the Palestinian policy is that it tries to implement a comprehensive, multistakeholder approach to reforming the land sector, including land use optimization, completeness of land registration, improved services to citizens, and efficient, transparent management of state land. Global experience in the modernization of land administration has shown that such a comprehensive approach and a long-term political commitment are prerequisites for success. Even with such an approach, however, adequate technical, financial, and operational capacity often remain hurdles that need to be addressed.

As for the legal frameworks, important challenges remain to bringing them in line with the need of modern economies, reducing the complexities of land tenure regimes, and promoting a convergence between the statutory and the customary legal regimes. Customary regimes are evolving with a trend toward the individualization/privatization of land. In Morocco, a process of "melkisation" has been in place since the late 1960s to convert collective rural land into individual private land (*melk*). So far, however, the process has had little success because of institutional coordination issues, difficulties addressing joint ownership, and the exclusion of women from being beneficiaries (as discussed later in this chapter). Another example of government policy to simplify tenure is the individualization/privatization of land such as Jordan's suppression in 2019 of the legal category of *miri* land (state land that carries private use rights) and its conversion into *mulk* land (private land). The main purpose was to facilitate real estate transactions in areas where cities had expanded and where major tribes had obtained such use rights.

Reforms are also needed to integrate the main land administration and management functions, which are currently fragmented. Integration of these functions leads to more consistent land information (harmonization of records) and more efficient service provision and use of government resources. Integration would also make it likelier that a self-funding model can be established. Countries that have made efforts to integrate the key responsibilities for land administration (that is, registration, cadaster, and valuation) are the GCC countries of Bahrain, Qatar, and the United Arab Emirates, as well as Jordan and Morocco. For example, in 2003 Bahrain merged its Survey Directorate with the Land Registration Bureau to oversee the land administration system. Jordan has long had a single agency that combines all these responsibilities.

Doing Business data suggest that institutional consolidation is associated with more efficient service delivery.[5] Egypt, for example, which has placed the cadaster, registry, and state land management functions in various institutions, ranks at the bottom with a registration time of 76 days. By contrast, in Jordan registration takes only 17 days.[6] Clearly, then, addressing institutional fragmentation in land administration and management produces strong gains, but in several countries in the MENA region institutional consolidation is a long-term agenda that requires a strong political commitment. Finding ways to incrementally streamline land management functions (such as simplifying procedures, establishing one-stop shops, and improving the interoperability of land information systems) can provide gains in the short term.

MOBILIZING REVENUE FROM LAND

Many MENA countries have considerable scope to leverage land for revenue generation through property taxation, but so far attempts to do so have faced resistance. Moving forward will require addressing technical and political obstacles—in particular, completing registries, developing a valuation infrastructure, improving tax administration capacity, and reducing tax exemptions to a minimum. In Morocco, where, besides Israel, property taxes constitute the highest percentage of GDP in the MENA region, the government is reluctant to increase the overall tax burden and has little appetite for property tax increases that cannot be offset by decreases in other taxes. Another example of such concerns is Egypt, which tried to increase its tax base in 2008 with a law establishing a fine for owners who failed to declare their property to the Real Estate Tax Authority.[7] Resistance to the law led to its postponement until 2014, when the exemption threshold was expanded. To mitigate shortfalls in property tax collection stemming from exemptions, the Real Estate Tax Authority has adopted a policy of targeting high-value properties such as offices and business parks, effectively creating a wealth tax instead of a nationwide property tax.

These examples highlight the difficulty of moving forward to expand property taxation in the MENA region. One of the key issues is the narrowness of the tax base arising from the low levels of registration, the numerous exemptions, and the lack of transparency, which generates mistrust, perceptions of unfairness, and lack of compliance. In the short term, countries can review and plan for expanding their tax bases, relying on better communication on tax reforms to improve public confidence in the tax, better targeting of tax exemptions and of tax relief beneficiaries (reducing them to the minimum), and increasing the capacity of the tax administration. In the longer term, improving registration will increase the tax base and make it possible to lower tax rates and have a fairer property taxation system based on market values.

Land market principles should be applied to land valuation and taxation, thereby increasing revenue generation and making the taxation system fairer. Instead, many governments in the region are currently basing taxation on book value (see chapter 2). Reforms to align property valuation with market values and reduce distortions from taxation exemptions (particularly on vacant land) are still needed in the region but are under consideration in only a few countries. In the West Bank and Gaza, the first steps are being taken to develop the infrastructure for property valuation based on market values. Lebanon is also considering a mass valuation system based on the country's underlying property market. In the short term, the priorities will be to build the skills and capacity for valuation, clarify the mandates of the institutions in charge, and align with internationally recognized standards for valuation. Countries can then begin to pilot the collection of land data and the development of land information systems that will allow both mass and individual valuations. Investments in valuation infrastructure will incur significant start-up costs, but they can have very large long-term, wide-ranging benefits for economies through better functioning of land and mortgage markets, better management of land, more productive public investments, fairer tax systems, greater transparency and accountability, and better revenue generation for governments.

Beyond property taxation, MENA countries could benefit from adopting a range of land value capture instruments. These instruments can provide financing options for infrastructure investments in ways that are efficient (they allow targeting the direct beneficiaries of investments by having them contribute in proportion to their benefits) and fair (with governments reclaiming some of the benefits of their own investments). In some MENA countries, laws already provide for a range of land value capture instruments such as betterment charges, development fees, and a land value increment tax (for example, in Egypt, Lebanon, and the West Bank and Gaza). However, it seems that these instruments are seldom implemented. For example, Egypt has had a betterment levy since 1955,[8] but only a few governorates have applied the levy. The main technical reasons are the difficulties of assessment of before and after values and the collection of the levy itself. Using such instruments will thus be a longer-term objective for countries that will first need to set up functional land valuation systems.

BETTER MANAGING PUBLIC LAND

MENA countries should develop policies that clarify the objectives to be achieved through public land management, pursue more efficient allocation and use of public land based on cost/benefit assessments, and use public land to generate revenue. The redistribution of public land to fulfill the social contract remains central in some MENA countries, often as a continuation of traditional allocation mechanisms. However, such land redistribution, which is very common in oil- and gas-producing countries, results in inefficient, unsustainable allocations that are not undertaken to satisfy land management or development objectives and may even raise social discontent. In Oman, for example, the rapid population growth beginning in the 1970s spurred the government's lottery policy, which grants every Omani citizen the right to enter the lottery and eventually receive use rights over a plot of land. The lottery policy has been criticized for contributing to unsustainable urban sprawl (particularly around the capital, Muscat), requiring car-based mobility (and thereby contributing to greenhouse gas emissions), and consuming large quantities of energy, material, and spatial resources.

The recommended approach to land management requires rethinking long-established practices that treat land as a free resource for redistribution or delivery of public services without considering the costs (economic, environmental, and social). It also requires treating public land and properties as a portfolio of assets to be optimized. Efficiently managing public land is all the more important because of the high level of state ownership and the scarcity of land in the MENA region. Those aiming to improve public land management should give priority to setting up or completing public land inventories as part of the development of land information management systems, while improving the asset management capacity of institutions. They also should adopt more transparent market-driven mechanisms of allocation such as auctions instead of lotteries or direct allocations. The latter are less efficient because they may fail to allocate land to the best use and diminish the potential for generating public revenue (see, for example, World Bank 2006a, 2006b). In the longer term, efficient management of public land will require better coordination of the institutions that control land and its allocation, as well as some level of decentralization of land management functions.

MENA countries should consider pursuing public-private partnerships (PPPs) for public land development or for land service delivery, which in some countries will require legislative reforms. This approach would help reduce inefficiencies, relieve financial constraints and increase access to capital, and lower a government's exposure to risk by sharing investment risks with the private sector. According to the Organisation for Economic Co-operation and Development (OECD), MENA countries generally do not resort to PPPs because of the high risk to the private sector of engaging in such arrangements. Factors include the absence of an adequate legal framework for PPPs, governments' lack of experience and expertise in setting up PPPs, and financial and contractual risks (OECD, n.d.). Moreover, the government land proposed for such projects may also not be optimally located, reducing the viability of projects and attractiveness of PPPs. Nevertheless, for countries that have in place the enabling environment for PPPs, there are successful examples of private sector leverage. A notable example is the United Arab Emirates, where the Dubai Land Department has partnered with dozens of private sector actors to advance real estate development initiatives and improve land registration services. For public services, the government has established the necessary enabling environment through its 2015 PPP Law, which provides a legal framework specifying policies and standards for private sector participation in public service provision.

MENA countries that have adopted desert land reclamation policies in response to land scarcity have to reassess whether these approaches are sustainable in the longer term. Desert land reclamation is a strategy used by MENA governments to meet growing demands for land (residential, industrial, and agricultural). Algeria, Egypt, Jordan, Morocco, and Saudi Arabia have reclaimed desert land for agriculture. Bahrain and Qatar have resorted to desert land reclamation for housing programs to accommodate urban population growth. In Egypt, desert land reclamation has been at the core of spatial development efforts that have for decades been using desert land for industrial zones and new cities (22 have been built so far and about 20 more are planned).[9]

This approach of growing into the desert has met limited success so far as industrial zones and new cities struggle to attract jobs and people (see the analysis in chapter 4). It has also raised concerns about the environmental externalities, the disconnect from integrated urban planning, the slow pace of spatial transformation generated by these massive investments, and the exclusion of the poorer segments of society.[10] In Jordan, the reclamation of arid and semiarid land has led to significant conflicts between the state and the local tribes who claim ownership of the land (Al Naber and Molle 2016). These challenges could be transitory because spatial transformation takes time, or they could linger because of lack of the required enabling environment (such as infrastructure connecting industrial zones in the desert to markets or connecting new cities to jobs, as analyzed in this report). They also reflect mistargeting, such as the choice of distant sites for industrial zones or the income levels of residents to be housed in new cities. The key issue is that land reclamation is often used to avoid resolving issues related to land speculation and the artificial land shortages in existing urban areas. It is much easier to construct new homes in the desert, where there are usually no ownership issues, than it is to resolve the structural issues that have contributed to land ownership challenges in existing cities. The choice to move forward with reclamation has resulted in urban sprawl and the higher energy and resource costs of providing the newly developed desert areas with services (Abubakar and Dano 2020).

Similarly, any MENA countries engaged in land reclamation from the sea in response to land scarcity should carefully evaluate the sustainability issues associated with this approach. The GCC countries have heavily invested in seaward land reclamation (that is, building artificial land surfaces in the sea offshore), often for specific development projects such as the Hassan II Mosque in Morocco and the Palm Islands in Dubai. However, although the artificial islands in both Dubai and Abu Dhabi have in the wake of declining oil reserves and revenue helped boost the real estate sector in the United Arab Emirates and diversify the economy such as through tourism, they raise environmental concerns. These concerns include coastal erosion from disrupted waterways and the negative impacts on marine biodiversity and ecosystems native to the coastline of both Emirates.

Overall, land reclamation policies in the MENA region, whether in the desert or in the sea, have not always had significant transformative impacts. Instead, they seem to be second-best substitutes for directly addressing key development issues in existing built-up areas. Those issues include upgrading informal areas, improving infrastructure, ensuring better service provision, and indirectly serving other economic objectives such as providing the upper and middle classes with savings opportunities through real estate investment, fostering employment in construction and real estate development, and generating public revenue. Land reclamation policies are also a suboptimal response to land shortages for development initiatives in view of their environmental impacts and the inefficiencies arising from urban sprawl, and they may offer poor returns to middle-class investors and the public exchequer. The resources used would be better directed toward investment in the existing built-up areas.

MANAGING AGRICULTURAL LAND: POLICIES AND STRATEGIC OBJECTIVES

In MENA countries, long-established policies serving food sovereignty and food security objectives have provided incentives to increase the use of land for domestic agricultural production in ways that are not sustainable and should be revisited. These policies have been adopted in a context of diminishing self-sufficiency[11] and vulnerability to the rising commodity price volatility in international markets. Meanwhile, these policies have contributed to increasing the quantity of land moved to cultivation and to shifting crop choices toward water-intense varieties, thereby exacerbating water depletion, land degradation, and other environmental consequences (Varis and Abu-Zeid 2009). In Egypt, for example, food self-sufficiency policies have led to the large water footprints stemming from the production of crops such as wheat that require large quantities of water (Abdelkader et al. 2018). A similar trend for wheat and other water-intensive crop production can be found in Tunisia and Morocco.[12] Because of predictions that the Arabian Aquifer System will be depleted within the next 3 to 14 decades (World Bank, forthcoming), an urgent regionwide response is needed to ensure more sustainable uses of land.

Meeting the food demand in more sustainable ways can be achieved through a combination of more efficient agricultural production at home and reliance on agricultural investments abroad and food imports from countries that face less land and water stress. In fact, the trend in the MENA region has long been one of increased reliance on imports. Its share of food sourced from the international market has increased fourfold, from 10 percent in 1961 to 40 percent half a century later, and it is expected to continue increasing (Le Mouël and Schmitt 2018).[13] Food imports make use of the resources of the exporting countries, thereby helping the MENA region save on its use of land and consumption of water.[14]

In most countries, little has been done to improve the sustainability of domestic production, with countries continuing to keep in place subsidies to water and agriculture. Nor have countries done much to mitigate the significant food waste in the region[15] or to improve the efficiency of food production,[16] which would increase food availability without exacerbating land and water consumption. These options would be much less costly and more sustainable than expanding production.

Saudi Arabia is the only country in the region to take drastic measures to address the sustainability of agricultural land use. In 2008, it enacted a ban on wheat production in an attempt to preserve its water resources.[17] The ban decreased the area under wheat production by more than 75 percent (and domestic production of wheat by the same proportion). It was implemented with acceptance of a dramatic increase in wheat imports (figure 5.2). However, the ban has since been partially reversed to accommodate small and medium-size farmers. The Saudi case demonstrates that taking such measures to reduce unsustainable land uses is an option, but it confirms that their social impacts or the opposition to them by affected groups must be addressed upon implementation. Because the relaxation occurred in a context in which oil revenue was tapering off, it highlights concerns about a policy choice that relies on a country's capacity to finance massive food imports over the long term.

Pressure to reduce food dependence has also motivated several countries to acquire or secure large tracts of land in Sub-Saharan African countries such as Ethiopia to produce commodities and export them back to the investor country (Arezki, Bogmans, and Selod 2018). These investments, however, have created tensions over access to land and water in the destination countries, particularly with local communities who often lack recognized property rights and may be forced off their land by the beneficiary governments in favor of foreign investments (Jägerskog and Kim 2016). In response to these concerns, the international community has come up with sets of principles to guide such investments in ways that will be more sustainable and respectful of the interests of local communities.[18]

Figure 5.2 Wheat harvested area and wheat imports, Saudi Arabia, 1961–2018

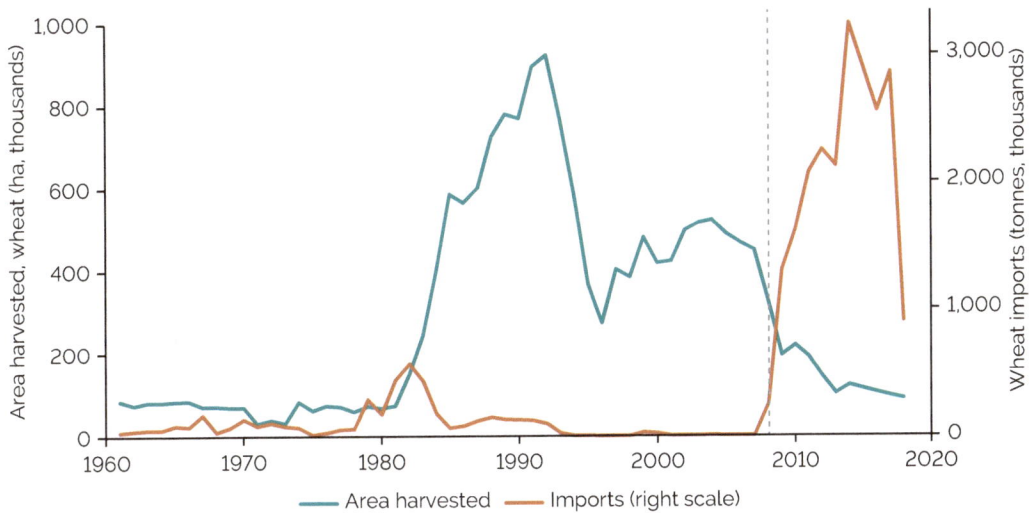

Source: Authors' calculations, based on Food and Agriculture Organization, FAOSTAT (dashboard), http://www.fao.org/faostat/.
Note: The vertical dashed line marks the 2008 enactment of a ban on wheat production. ha = hectares.

Whether and the extent to which agricultural land should be preserved or desert land should be reclaimed for agriculture are important policy questions for several countries in the MENA region because of the cost of these policies and the pace of climate-induced land degradation. In peri-urban areas, tensions have emerged from the conversion of peri-urban agricultural land into urban land, with some governments taking action to protect agricultural land. This approach implicitly assumes that land markets do not produce a socially desirable outcome by valuing residential use over agricultural use. The benefits and costs of land conversion should be assessed and should drive policy objectives and land planning decisions. Leapfrogging urban expansion into the desert helps preserve scarce peri-urban agricultural land and contain congestion in the existing cities, but it has economic, social, and environmental costs that should be assessed. Land reclamation for urban development as well as agriculture is still very much on the agenda of a country like Egypt—its 2015 National Project for Reclamation and Cultivation aims to increase farmland by 20 percent. However, past experiences have shown that such initiatives not only are very costly but also increase stress on water, and fuel tensions on access to water.[19] In view of the projected impacts of climate change and uncontrolled urban expansion, it is unlikely that land reclamation will be able to reverse the trend of long-term desertification and land degradation.

The present trends in land and water scarcity suggest that MENA countries need to come to terms with their growing dependency on food imports and set up adequate mechanisms to manage related vulnerabilities. To be sustained over the long term, increased food imports will have to be accompanied by measures that ensure both financial and social feasibility. To pay for growing food imports, countries will have to generate more income through exports and prioritize economic diversification. Because reliance on imports involves vulnerability to shocks affecting international production and the prices of agricultural commodities, safety nets in the form of cash transfers or in-kind support could help protect the poor from such shocks. Strategic storage of agricultural produce, although costly, could also help countries smooth global shocks to agricultural production.

Agricultural land fragmentation stemming from land redistribution policies or the division of parcels following inheritance remains a pervasive problem in the MENA region, especially in Algeria, Egypt, Morocco, and Tunisia. The current policies pursuing land consolidation through cooperatives have had mixed success because of unresolved social, legal, technical, and capacity constraints. Other policy options such as land banking, which proved successful in other contexts, should be considered. Some countries have tried to address fragmentation by pooling land in cooperatives that can achieve economies of scale in agricultural production. In the Islamic Republic of Iran, for example, government policy has sought to encourage the creation of farmer cooperatives through awareness campaigns and financial incentives.[20] However, the success of the cooperatives has been limited due to socioeconomic and technical constraints, including the reluctance of farmers to relinquish their access to land, especially plots they inherited, as well as the difficult implementation of land consolidation in certain regions because water consolidation is not considered in the design (Abdollahzadeh et al. 2012; Shetty 2006).

Notably, in the MENA region consolidation has not been pursued at scale using complementary instruments that could serve as intermediaries in the process of land pooling. One example is land banks, which have proven to be relatively successful in other contexts, such as in some Eastern European countries in the postsocialist period. Other attempts to mitigate land fragmentation in the MENA region have involved legislative approaches to avoid excessive fragmentation. For example, Morocco has established limits to land partition with a minimum of 5 hectares within irrigated perimeters. Outside the region, a similar approach was implemented by Turkey, whose Soil Conservation and Land Use Law establishes a minimum farm size and forbids subdivision of land under the threshold by inheritance or sale. The Turkish approach has proven to be somewhat successful—an estimated 700,000 hectares were not subjected to subdivision, and 6.4 million parcels were transferred to heirs without subdivision (FAO 2014). All these approaches to address fragmentation focus on facilitating land mobility. They could be accompanied by interventions to ensure that holders of land have alternative opportunities for income generation that provide them with incentives to rent out or sell their land rather than hold on to it.

RESPONDING TO URBAN LAND NEEDS

Better land governance and more efficient mobilization of public land are needed to stimulate land markets and increase the formal supply of land for urban development. Mobilizing public land will require a clear policy on public land management, identifying the best potential use of the stock of public land and efficient ways to make some of this stock available for investment. At the same time, the stock of public land in locations suitable for urban development has been decreasing, indicating that the traditional model of relying on public land for urban development is facing serious challenges. In many instances, the diminished availability of public land has resulted in suboptimal location choices for urban development, particularly for affordable housing (such as in Iraq, Jordan, and Saudi Arabia) and slum relocation interventions (such as in Egypt, Morocco, and Tunisia). This situation has contributed to inefficient spatial development. Affordable housing programs have been forced to locate at the city periphery without connection to the infrastructure grid, further exacerbating spatial sprawl, service delivery difficulties, and the strains on transport systems and giving rise to harmful impacts on the environment. In addition, the tendency to opt for spatially suboptimal choices circumvents the difficult resolution of land tenure issues in the existing cities, leading to a preference for new developments over upgrading. To overcome these challenges, MENA governments will have to find alternative models that can mobilize to a greater extent private land for urban development. This will require major improvements in land governance to clarify land tenure situations and property rights, establish the appropriate infrastructure for market valuation of land, and address idle land. These measures are necessary not only to stimulate the formal land supply to respond to urban needs, but also to ensure that land conversion processes for urban use become more transparent and fairer.

Tailored approaches are needed to address the common issue of vacant land. Several countries in the region face the paradox of having both a significant amount of undeveloped land in their cities and a housing shortage. In fact, vacant land has exacerbated land shortages in urban areas, which has resulted in spikes in real estate prices (see, for example, the case of Ramallah in the West Bank). Saudi Arabia, facing a similar issue, is addressing it through taxation of vacant land (see the analysis in chapter 4). Other GCC countries are following or planning to follow suit (Kuwait and Oman).

Several countries in the region also face a problem of vacant residential units. In Jordan, this phenomenon is partly due to current tax policies that levy lower real estate taxes on vacant residential units, which may have contributed to an estimated vacancy rate of 18 percent for the country's housing supply (World Bank 2018). A harmonization of the tax rates for vacant and occupied units (with vacant units taxed at the same or a higher rate than occupied units) is thus needed and should be feasible in the short run. However, the taxation of vacant land and vacant residential units faces strong opposition. A tax on vacant residential properties was envisioned in Egypt, but it was deemed unconstitutional by the Supreme Court with the argument that the tax was too high and would be equivalent to a form of confiscation.[21]

Overcoming opposition to the taxation of vacant land or vacant residential units will require better communication with the general public and state authorities on the public benefits and fairness of the taxation approach to reduce vacancies. And yet tax penalties can be difficult to apply where there is lack of clarity on land ownership and the tax administration lacks capacity. In the case of vacant land, even when feasible, tax penalties may not be sufficient to incentivize construction because other obstacles may be hindering real estate development such as difficulty obtaining building permits or lack of funding for real estate development. Addressing these other causes of vacant land would require other land governance interventions—among them, improvements in land use regulations to encourage infill, in land administration to reduce the costs associated with real estate transfers and development, and in urban land planning more generally, including better management of public land in prime locations. Other interventions outside the land sector could also help reduce vacant land. For example, macroeconomic policies that stimulate credit, attract investment, or provide alternative savings options to households would encourage construction and deter speculative landholdings. A policy approach combining these fiscal and regulatory instruments is likely to be more effective.

Increasing the formal land supply and enabling formal land markets to function more efficiently will also be required to improve firms' access to land. Governments in the MENA region have adopted various approaches to facilitating access to land in zones where firms can cluster. In Egypt, for example, the government has been promoting industrial zones since the late 1980s, but with nuanced results. The creation of industrial zones on public land has responded to some extent to firms' difficulties to accessing formal land of sufficient area at a reasonable cost, but more successful implementation will require better locations (see the analysis in chapter 4), better service infrastructure, and better management of such zones, including through PPPs. Beyond mobilizing land for economic clusters, interventions to clarify property rights and simplify land administration procedures for firms to access land should remain a key complementary priority.

PROMOTING EQUAL ACCESS TO LAND FOR WOMEN AND VULNERABLE GROUPS

Gender equality in land rights has been promoted internationally and has inspired initiatives in the region, but examples remain limited. Since the 1960s, improving women's land and property rights has been an integral aspect of efforts by the international community to reduce poverty and economically empower women in the MENA region (OHCHR and UN Women 2013). In 2000, the United Nations Human Rights Committee adopted General Comment No. 28 entitled "Equality of Rights Between Men and Women." An amendment to Article 3 of the 1966 International Covenant on Civil and Political Rights, it obligates states to ensure the equality of women's inheritance rights (COHRE 2006). The 1995 Beijing Declaration and Platform for Action at the Fourth Conference for Women called for states to "give women full and equal access to economic resources, including the right to inheritance and to ownership of land and property." These initiatives have been the backbone of legislative reform efforts, including in Tunisia. In fact, in 2018 the president of Tunisia proposed, at the recommendation of the high-level Committee on Personal Freedoms and Equality (Colibe), a draft law establishing parity between women and men in matters of inheritance. Although approved by the cabinet in November 2018, it faced strong political opposition and was not enacted into law (Tanner 2020).

Countries that have made progress have done so under pressure from civil society, but taking gradual steps. Responding to calls from some segments of civil society, many countries have adopted measures to ensure that women have better access to land and enjoy strong property rights. For example, in Tunisia debates over ensuring equality in inheritance shares have been at the forefront of civil discussions over the last 10 years (Euro-Mediterranean Women's Foundation 2018). In 2011 Jordan introduced legislative amendments to establish a three-month "cooling-off period" following registration of inheritance shares during which renunciation of rights is not allowed (see chapter 3). In Egypt, following a massive years-long campaign by civil society actors, family courts were finally instituted in 2004 to provide a one-stop shop for family issues and personal status cases, including property and inheritance cases (see box 5.1). In 2005, Algeria modified its personal family code to allow women to confer their citizenship on their children, with implications for the inheritance of land and property and access to finance. In Morocco, the Soulalyat movement has achieved many notable legislative reforms in favor of women, such as the formal recognition of women as beneficiaries of compensation following the transfer of collective land (see box 5.2). Finally, in the Islamic Republic of Iran a dynamic interpretation of the law by the Supreme Leader of the Islamic Revolution in 2009 enabled the reform of the Civil Code to give women the right to inherit land (see box 5.3).

Box 5.1 Inheritance reform in the Arab Republic of Egypt

In December 2017, the Egyptian Parliament took the lead in supporting women's rights to inheritance in the MENA region. It approved two amendments to the Inheritance Law (No. 77 of 1943) that punish those who deliberately prevent heirs (and, in particular, women) from receiving their share of inheritance. Punishment is imprisonment for six months and a fine of LE 20,000–100,000—or US$1,200–$6,000 (ECWR 2017). This positive change stems from a two-year campaign led by the National Council for Women, including the Egyptian Feminist Union and the New Woman Association, to inform 1.2 million rural women who had been deprived of inheritance of their rights. The *Tareq al-Abwab* (Door-Knocking) campaign was part of the National Strategy for the Empowerment of Egyptian Women 2030, launched in 2017 by Egypt's National Council for Women.

Source: OECD, ILO, and CAWTAR (2020).

Box 5.2 The Soulalyat mobilization for collective rural land in Morocco

In Morocco, an unprecedented social mobilization of rural women–the Soulalyat–began as an effort to obtain equal rights to inheritance. It has resulted in establishment of a program to legally transfer collective land to women. Prior to 2007, collective land belonged to kinship groups and thus could not be sold. The right to use the land for agriculture and to benefit from its proceeds, however, was customarily transferred from father to son. Because 42 percent of the land in Morocco—12 million hectares—was at the time governed by customary law, this practice carried important economic weight. The gendered nature of collective land governance left women excluded from compensation, and widows and unmarried women were especially vulnerable.

Several years of educational campaigns and protests in regions such as Rabat and Kenitra and support from the Democratic Association of Moroccan Women were needed to change public opinion about female inheritance rights. In 2009, the government adopted two circulars to consider women as beneficiaries of collective land. In 2012, women's rights to land ownership were extended to nontransferred land. Finally, in August 2019 Law 62-17 was passed to address the land owned by tribal "ethnic" communities. The new law affirmed women's rights to benefit from their ancestral lands alongside men. Approval of the law cemented an important step in the fight for gender equality in land rights that lasted over a decade. So far only 128 hectares have been distributed to 867 women, who have since maintained control over the land.

Sources: El Kirat el Allame (2020); Naciri (2020).

Box 5.3 Inheritance reform in the Islamic Republic of Iran

In May 2009, the Iranian Parliament amended Article 949 of the Civil Code to give women the right to inherit land and removed the limits on the proportion of movable property a woman could inherit. Until 2009, women heirs could be compensated for the value of "land and trees" but could not inherit land itself—a provision initially intended to keep land within families in case mothers remarried. Because of opposition from religious figures who found the amendment incompatible with Islam, the Iranian Parliament passed the new law only after the Guardian Council of the Islamic Revolution requested a religious opinion (*fatwa*) from the Supreme Leader of the Islamic Revolution. Because he favored this new dynamic interpretation (*ijtihad*) of the law, Ayatollah Khamenei passed the *fatwa*, and the Parliament was able to approve the amendment requested by civil society.

Source: US Library of Congress, "Iran: New Women's Inheritance Law Is Enforced," https://www.loc.gov/item/global-legal -monitor/2009-05-15/iran-new-womens-inheritance-law-is-enforced/#:~:text=%28May%2015%2C%202009%29%20The%20 Iranian%20government%20has%20begun,to%20inherit%20all%20forms%20of%20their%20husband%27s%20property.

Policies aimed at narrowing the gender gap in accessing land can play an important role in addressing the broader systemic gender imbalances in the region. However, although successful initiatives for change and policy reform have emerged throughout the MENA region, they are often promoted by either small sections of civil society or a subset of government actors and generally lack support from all segments of society. In fact, in most countries the majority of civil society is in favor of the application of *shari'a* law, which is viewed as supportive of women and women's rights. As a result, most activists must work with religious authorities to implement *shari'a* law in matters of inheritance.

In addition, reforms are often contingent on the recommendations issued by the Arab Charter on Human Rights (endorsed by the Arab League in 1994), which protects the rights to equality for all "in the framework of the positive discrimination established in favor of women by the Islamic Law" (COHRE 2006). According to the Committee on the Elimination of Discrimination against Women (CEDAW), moving forward it will be necessary to "put in place, without delay, a comprehensive strategy to modify or eliminate patriarchal attitudes and stereotypes that discriminate against women. Such measures should include efforts, in collaboration with civil society and community and religious leaders, to educate and raise awareness regarding the substantive equality of women and men and should target women and men at all levels of society" (CEDAW 2017). Policies such as those implemented in Tunisia and Jordan that directly address discrepancies in land and property inheritance could be replicated in countries throughout the region to improve equitable access to land. Because of opposition to such reforms, another option is to use land policies to reduce gender inequalities even if that does not directly address land access discrepancies. For example, one approach could be to tax the male beneficiaries of female renunciation of land in order to fund initiatives promoting women empowerment (through, for example, access to education and health).

ANNEX 5A: TAXONOMY OF MENA COUNTRIES—LAND ISSUES

The analysis in this report has revealed that MENA countries both share commonalities and differ according to their economic, institutional, geographic, and demographic contexts. These dimensions can be captured for each country by applying the following relevant indicators: national wealth (measured by the gross domestic product per capita), the quality of land institutions (measured by the Doing Business indicator Quality of Land Administration), the gender gap (measured by UNDP's Gender Inequality Index), demographic pressure (measured by the expected percentage increase in population by 2050), and land scarcity (measured by the amount of cropland per capita viewed from space and reported in the MODIS land cover data, as well as by the per capita amount of grassland that could be turned into rainfed agriculture). Table 5A.1 presents the country values for these indicators.

Table 5A.1 Selected indicators, MENA

Country/ economy	GDP per capita (US$)	Quality of Land Administration	Gender Inequality Index	Expected population growth by 2050 (%)	Cropland per capita (ha)	Per capita uncultivated land suitable for rainfed agriculture (ha)
Algeria	4,154	7.5	0.443	32.5	0.145	0.047
Bahrain	23,991	19.5	0.207	37.1	0.000	0.000
Djibouti	3,142	7.0	0.421	30.8	0.000	0.000
Egypt, Arab Rep.	2,537	9.0	0.450	49.0	0.033	0.000
Iran, Islamic Rep.	3,598	16.0	0.492	11.9	0.087	0.018
Iraq	5,523	10.5	0.540	96.3	0.115	0.019
Israel	41,705	22.5	0.100	44.3	0.059	0.023

Continued

Table 5A.1 Selected indicators, MENA *(continued)*

Country/ economy	GDP per capita (US$)	Quality of Land Administration	Gender Inequality Index	Expected population growth by 2050 (%)	Cropland per capita (ha)	Per capita uncultivated land suitable for rainfed agriculture (ha)
Jordan	4,308	22.5	0.469	39.0	0.026	0.001
Kuwait	33,399	18.5	0.245	31.2	0.000	0.000
Lebanon	8,013	16.0	0.362	–10.1	0.029	0.011
Libya	7,877	7.0	0.172	21.9	0.175	0.007
Malta	30,672	12.5	0.195	–3.5	0.000	0.005
Morocco	3,227	17.0	0.492	23.2	0.223	0.029
Oman	16,521	17.0	0.304	31.2	0.004	0.000
Qatar	65,908	26.0	0.202	35.2	0.000	0.000
Saudi Arabia	23,337	14.0	0.224	29.8	0.011	0.000
Syrian Arab Republic	2,378	8.5	0.547	79.8	0.219	0.025
Tunisia	3,439	13.5	0.300	16.6	0.226	0.012
United Arab Emirates	43,839	21.0	0.113	34.1	0.000	0.000
West Bank and Gaza	3,562	13.5	0.457	82.3	0.038	0.016
Yemen, Rep.	824	7.0	0.834	59.7	0.011	0.000
MENA country average	*15,807*	*14.6*	*0.360*	*36.8*	*0.067*	*0.010*
Standard deviation	*17,552*	*5.6*	*0.175*	*25.5*	*0.080*	*0.013*

Sources: World Bank, World Development Indicators (database), https://databank.worldbank.org/source/world-development-indicators; World Bank, Doing Business 2004–2020 (database), https://archive.doingbusiness.org/en/doingbusiness; United Nations Development Programme, Human Development Reports, Gender Inequality Index (GII) (dashboard), https://hdr.undp.org/en/content/gender-inequality-index-gii; United Nations, Department of Economic and Social Affairs, World Urbanization Prospects 2018 (dashboard), https://population.un.org/wup/; MODIS Land Cover Type (MCD12Q1) version 6, https://lpdaac.usgs.gov/products/mcd12q1v006/; Food and Agriculture Organization, GAEZ-FAO V4.0, https://gaez.fao.org.

Note: GDP per capita is in 2018 current US dollars. In the absence of data for Syria since 2007, the nominal 2007 Syrian GDP per capita converted to 2018 US dollars is used. In the 2020 Doing Business data set, Libya is scored "No practice" for its Quality of Land Administration. Libya's score was reconstructed by allotting it a score of 7, corresponding to the lowest score in the sample equal to that of Djibouti or the Republic of Yemen. Because the value for the 2020 Gender Inequality Index for the West Bank and Gaza is missing, it was reconstructed by applying the methodology described in the Technical Notes attached to *Human Development Report 2020*, using the raw data from statistical annex table 5 of the *Human Development Report* and accounting for a share of women in Parliament of 12.9 percent. The value of the Gender Inequality Index for Djibouti was also reconstructed using the completion rate for lower-secondary education by gender for 2006—the only year for which these data are available—instead of the percentage of the population with at least some secondary education by gender, which is used to calculate the indicator for the other countries but is not available for Djibouti for any year. The estimation of cropland per capita and of per capita uncultivated land suitable for rainfed agriculture is described in annex 1A. ha = hectares.

A taxonomy of MENA countries along these indicators was obtained by running a principal component analysis using the data in table 5A.1. The analysis led to the selection of two components accounting for 70 percent of the variation in the data.[22] A varimax rotation was performed to facilitate interpretation of the components, and the "loadings" of the two rotated components on the six variables are presented in table 5A.2. Retaining loadings values above 0.3 for the interpretation, a clear interpretation of each component emerges. By negatively loading GDP per capita and the Quality of Land Administration and positively loading the Gender Inequality Index, component 1 differentiates between poorer countries with weaker governance and richer countries with stronger governance. With a positive loading on expected population growth, component 1 can thus be interpreted as measuring weak governance and demographic pressure. With strong positive loadings for cropland per capita and per capita uncultivated land suitable for rainfed agriculture, component 2 clearly measures agricultural land availability—an inverse measure of land scarcity. Figure 5.1 earlier in this chapter shows the country score plots on these two components and forms the basis of the country typology.[23]

Table 5A.2 Component loadings

Indicator	Component 1 "Weak governance and demographic pressure"	Component 2 "Land availability for rainfed agriculture"	Share of unexplained variation
GDP per capita	**−.501**	−.161	.22
Quality of Land Administration	**−.477**	−.087	.37
Gender Inequality Index	**.595**	−.085	.21
Expected population growth by 2050	**.409**	−.175	.65
Cropland per capita	.024	**.683**	.15
Per capita uncultivated land suitable for rainfed agriculture	−.024	**.680**	.22

Source: World Bank. See table 5A.1 for data sources.
Note: Loadings greater than 0.3 in absolute value are shown in boldface and used for the interpretation of the components.

NOTES

1. World Bank, Doing Business 2004–2020 (database), https://archive.doingbusiness.org/en/doingbusiness; United Nations Development Programme, Human Development Reports, Gender Inequality Index (GII) (dashboard), https://hdr.undp.org/en/content/gender-inequality-index-gii; United Nations, Department of Economic and Social Affairs, World Urbanization Prospects 2018 (dashboard), https://population.un.org/wup/.

2. MODIS Land Cover Type (MCD12Q1) version 6, https://lpdaac.usgs.gov/products/mcd12q1v006/; Food and Agriculture Organization, FAO Global Agro-Ecological Zones (GAEZ) V4.0, https://gaez.fao.org/. See annex 1A for explanations about how the remaining land suitable for cultivation was measured.

3. More than 800,000 titles have been registered. They cover 13 percent of the territory used—the rest is desert land.

4. Cabinet Decision No. 01/171/2017.

5. World Bank, Doing Business 2004–2020 (database), https://archive.doingbusiness.org/en/doingbusiness.

6. In 2002, Morocco also placed a single agency in charge of registration, cadaster, and mapping (Agence Nationale de la Conservation Foncière, du Cadastre et de la Cartographie). Similarly, and to address rapid urbanization

soon after its discovery of oil, in 1972 Oman quickly developed land administration processes and delegated sole responsibility for its land management to the Ministry of Land Affairs (now the Ministry of Housing and Urban Development).

7. Law 196/2008.

8. Betterment Levy Law 222 of 1955.

9. Although not explicitly stated, land reclamation in Egypt is also a means of generating revenue through the sale of public land.

10. The impact on water is of particular concern because of the higher demand on Nile water and on groundwater (Switzman, Coulibaly, and Adeel 2015).

11. MENA countries are expected to import up to 60–70 percent of their food by 2050 (see Le Mouël and Schmitt 2018).

12. In the MENA region, the decrease in water availability (mainly because of agriculture) is dramatic. Whereas the availability of freshwater was 4,000 cubic meters per capita in 1950, it is estimated to fall to 200 cubic meters per capita in two-thirds of countries in the region by 2040–50 (Antonelli and Tamea 2015).

13. Le Mouël and Schmitt (2018) predict that half the cultivable land in the Maghreb will disappear by 2040–50 and that, by the same time, 70 percent of the food consumption of the Maghreb countries will come from imports.

14. For example, a study revealed that Egypt's annual imports of 8.3 million tons of wheat contributed to "savings" of 1.3 million hectares of land and 7.5 billion cubic meters of irrigation water over the 2000–2012 period.

15. About one-third of all the food produced in the Near East and North Africa (NENA) region (which includes Sudan and Mauritania) is lost or wasted annually (FAO 2017).

16. By, for example, upgrading grain storage facilities or cold chains for perishable products.

17. Saudi Arabia had engaged in large-scale wheat production to serve its self-sufficiency objective and to diversify its revenue from oil by exporting wheat (a strategy pursued in the 1990s when oil prices were low). That production was organized by a state agency until 2016. In 2008, after a decade of oil price increases, the country reversed its policy to gradually ban production to preserve water. The ban, which was accompanied by compensation for farmers financed by oil revenues, called for phasing out domestic wheat production by 2016; abolishing import tariffs on cereals, animal feed, and wheat flour; and reducing the general tariff on foodstuffs from 75 percent to 5 percent (Napoli et al. 2016).

18. See, in particular, the *Principles for Responsible Agricultural Investment that Respects Rights, Livelihoods and Resources* (FAO et al. 2010); the *Voluntary Guidelines on the Responsible Governance of Tenure of Land, Fisheries and Forests in the Context of National Food Security* (FAO 2012); and the *Principles for Responsible Investments in Agriculture and Food Systems* (FAO 2014).

19. Land reclamation began in Egypt in the 1930s. Land reclamation in the Sinai Peninsula during the 1980s and 1990s led to the diversion of water from the Nile, thereby reducing the water available to farmers in the Nile Delta (Wichelns 2002).

20. To encourage land consolidation, the government finances the necessary studies, including land consolidation design, as well as land leveling and infrastructure such as roads and irrigation networks.

21. Law 34 of 1978, which was deemed unconstitutional by the Supreme Court in 1993.

22. Components are a linear combination of variables (in this case the six indicators in table 5A.1), which are optimally chosen to explain the maximum variation in the data.

23. Robustness checks were performed by running principal component analyses with other variables correlated with the selection of variables (using the Property Rights score of the Bertelsmann Transformation Index in lieu of the Doing Business Quality of Land Administration score). This process produced very similar results in terms of component interpretation and groupings of countries.

REFERENCES

Abdelkader, A., A. Elshorbagy, M. Tuninetti, F. Laio, L. F. G. G. M. Ridolfi, H. Fahmy, and A. Y. Hoekstra. 2018. "National Water, Food, and Trade Modeling Framework: The Case of Egypt." *Science of the Total Environment* 639: 485–96.

Abdollahzadeh, G., K. Kalantari, A. Sharifzadeh, and A. Sehat. 2012. "Farmland Fragmentation and Consolidation Issues in Iran: An Investigation from Landholder's Viewpoint." *Journal of Agricultural Science and Technology* 14 (7): 1441–52.

Abubakar, I. R., and U. L. Dano. 2020. "Sustainable Urban Planning Strategies for Mitigating Climate Change in Saudi Arabia." *Environment, Development and Sustainability* 22 (6): 5129–52.

Al Naber, M., and F. Molle. 2016. "The Politics of Accessing Desert Land in Jordan." *Land Use Policy* 59: 492–503.

Antonelli, M., and S. Tamea. 2015. "Food-Water Security and Virtual Water Trade in the Middle East and North Africa." *International Journal of Water Resources Development* 31 (3): 326–42.

Arezki, M. R., M. C. Bogmans, and M. H. Selod. 2018. "The Globalization of Farmland: Theory and Empirical Evidence." Policy Research Working Paper 8456, World Bank, Washington, DC.

CEDAW (Committee on the Elimination of Discrimination against Women). 2017. "Concluding Observations on the Sixth Periodic Report of Jordan." Office of the United Nations High Commissioner on Human Rights, Geneva. https://www.refworld.org/docid/596f495b4.html.

COHRE (Centre on Housing Rights and Evictions). 2006. "In Search of Equality: A Survey of Law and Practice Related to Women's Inheritance Rights in the Middle East and North Africa (MENA) Region." COHRE, Geneva.

ECWR (Egyptian Center for Women's Rights). 2017. "ECWR Welcomes the Amendment of the Inheritance Law." November 27, 2017. http://ecwronline.org/?p=7509.

El Kirat el Allame, Y. 2020. "Gender Matters: Women as Actors of Change and Sustainable Development in Morocco." In *Women's Grassroots Mobilization in the MENA Region Post-2011*, edited by K. P. Norman. Baker Institute for Public Policy, Rice University, Houston, TX.

Euro-Mediterranean Women's Foundation. 2018. *Report of the Committee on Personal Freedoms and Equality.* Barcelona: Committee on Personal Freedoms and Equality (Colibe).

FAO (Food and Agriculture Organization). 2012. *Voluntary Guidelines on the Responsible Governance of Tenure of Land, Fisheries and Forests in the Context of National Food Security.* Rome: FAO.

FAO (Food and Agriculture Organization). 2014. *Principles for Responsible Investment in Agriculture and Food Systems.* Rome: FAO.

FAO (Food and Agriculture Organization). 2017. *Near East and North Africa Regional Overview of Food Insecurity 2016.* Cairo: FAO.

FAO (Food and Agriculture Organization), IFAD (International Fund for Agricultural Development), UNCTAD (United Nations Conference on Trade and Development), and World Bank Group. 2010. *Principles for Responsible Agricultural Investment that Respects Rights, Livelihoods, and Resources.* Washington, DC: World Bank.

Jägerskog, A., and K. Kim. 2016. "Land Acquisition: A Means to Mitigate Water Scarcity and Reduce Conflict?" *Hydrological Sciences Journal* 61 (7): 1338–45.

Le Mouël, C., and B. Schmitt, eds. 2018. *Food Dependency in the Middle East and North Africa Region: Retrospective Analysis and Projections to 2050.* New York: Springer.

Naciri, R. 2020. "The Moroccan Soulalyat Movement: A Story of Exclusion and Empowerment." In *Women's Grassroots Mobilization in the MENA Region Post-2011*, edited by K. P. Norman. Baker Institute for Public Policy, Rice University, Houston, TX.

Napoli, C., B. Wise, D. Wogan, and L. Yaseen. 2016. "Policy Options for Reducing Water for Agriculture in Saudi Arabia." KASPARC Discussion Paper KS-1630-DP024A, King Abdullah Petroleum Studies and Research Center, Riyadh, Saudi Arabia.

OECD (Organisation for Economic Co-operation and Development). No date. "Public-Private Partnerships in the Middle East and North Africa: A Handbook for Policy Makers." OECD, Paris.

OECD (Organisation for Economic Co-operation and Development), ILO (International Labour Organization), and CAWTAR (Centre of Arab Women for Training and Research). 2020. *Changing Laws and Breaking Barriers for Women's Economic Empowerment in Egypt, Jordan, Morocco and Tunisia.* Paris: OECD Publishing. https://doi.org/10.1787/ac780735-en.

OHCHR (Office of the High Commissioner for Human Rights) and UN Women. 2013. *Realizing Women's Rights to Land and Other Productive Resources.* New York: United Nations.

Shetty, S. 2006. *Water, Food Security and Agricultural Policy in the Middle East and North Africa Region.* Washington, DC: World Bank.

Switzman, H., P. Coulibaly, and Z. Adeel. 2015. "Modeling the Impacts of Dryland Agricultural Reclamation on Groundwater Resources in Northern Egypt Using Sparse Data." *Journal of Hydrology* 520: 420–38.

Tanner, V. 2020. "Developing Alternatives. Strengthening Women's Control over Land: Inheritance Reform in Tunisia." DAI, Bethesda, MD. https://dai-global-developments.com/articles/strengthening-womens-control -over-land-inheritance-reform-in-tunisia.

USAID (US Agency for International Development). 2018. "USAID Country Profile—Property Rights and Resource Governance—Jordan." https://www.land-links.org/wp-content/uploads/2018/06/USAID_Land_Tenure _Profile_Jordan.pdf.

Varis, O., and K. Abu-Zeid. 2009. "Socio-economic and Environmental Aspects of Water Management in the 21st Century: Trends, Challenges and Prospects for the MENA Region." *International Journal of Water Resources Development* 25 (3): 507–22.

Wichelns, D. 2002. "An Economic Perspective on the Potential Gains from Improvements in Irrigation Water Management." *Agricultural Water Management* 52 (3): 233–48.

World Bank. 2006a. *Egypt Public Land Management Strategy. Volume I: Policy Note.* Washington, DC: World Bank.

World Bank. 2006b. *Egypt Public Land Management Strategy. Volume II: Background Notes on Access to Public Land by Investment Sector: Industry, Tourism, Agriculture and Real Estate Development.* Washington, DC: World Bank.

World Bank. 2018. "Jordan Housing Sector Review." World Bank, Washington, DC.

World Bank. Forthcoming. *Economics of Water Scarcity in MENA: Institutional Solutions.* Washington, DC: World Bank.

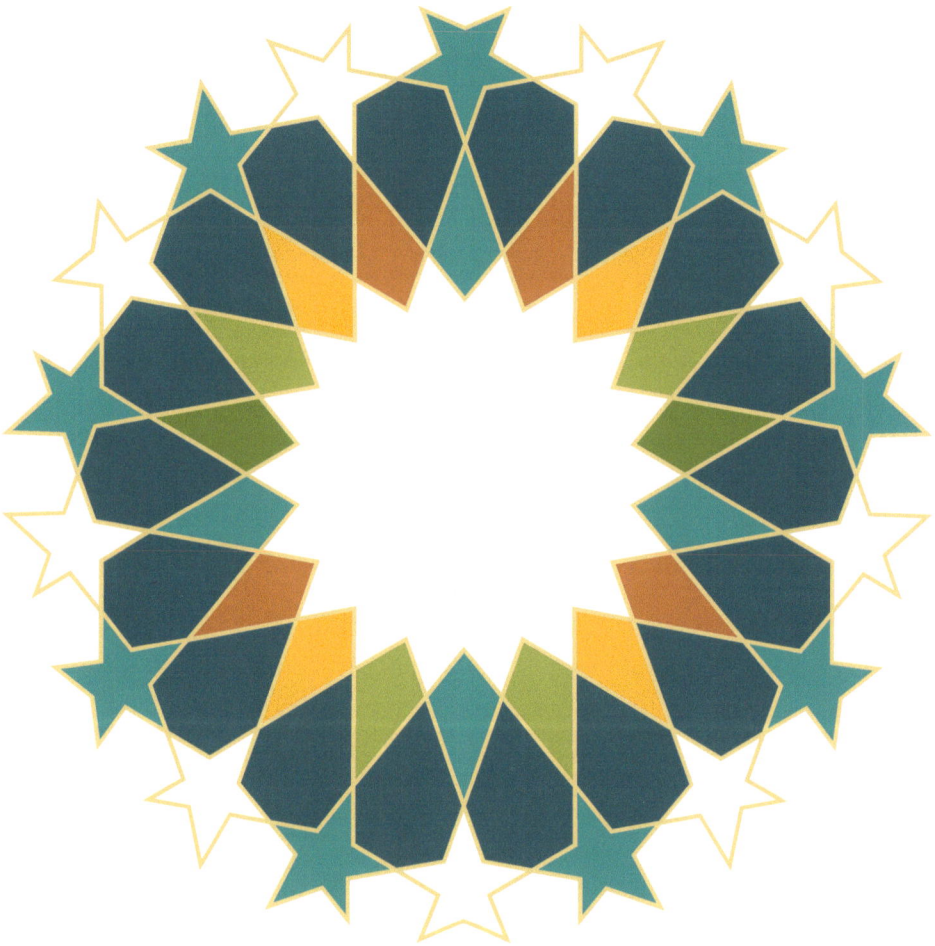

Conclusion and Priorities for Reform

In the MENA region, land, a key economic asset, is scarce and under stress from growing populations, urban expansion, and the impacts of climate change and conflicts. Weak land governance not only prevents the efficient use of the land, but also is costly and holds back the economy. Moreover, it inhibits strategic decisions about the trade-offs needed to ensure sustainable land use while responding to population needs such as housing and food security. The present economic and social inequalities are reflected in the persistent difficulties faced by women and vulnerable groups in accessing land.

A priority for intervention is modernization of land administration, including through digitization and improved transparency of information on land. Technology is important because of the scope for digital transformation in the region and the opportunities technology offers for cost-effective solutions, data generation and sharing, service delivery, and transparency, all of which are crucially lacking in the region. Moreover, as MENA governments consider new technologies, such as Smart City applications and the Internet of Things, to provide their citizens and businesses with better services and infrastructure, they will have to keep in mind that accurate, reliable geospatial information will be the cornerstone of any successful initiative. Complete textual and cadastral land records, as well as comprehensive legal and institutional frameworks that promote tenure security, will help government officials and key stakeholders make informed decisions about Smart City initiatives such as the development of business innovation hubs or green transportation corridors, while ensuring that the rights of land and property owners are protected. However, if land tenure insecurity challenges are not addressed, the ability to generate the foundational geospatial information required for Smart City initiatives and benefits for citizens and businesses across the MENA region will be severely limited.

Reforms needed in the land sector are not limited to land administration and land governance. They should also include the issues surrounding sustainability, strategic use of land assets, and access to land for vulnerable groups. All of these policy interventions have to some degree distributional impacts, with potential winners and losers. Sometimes, those opposing reforms in the land sector are the institutions themselves, fearing that they would lose power and influence (involving, in some instances, the loss of opportunities to extract rents, but also the possibility of job losses). Meanwhile, research has revealed that vested interests can prevent reforms and that political regimes drive the type of reforms undertaken. Along these lines, researchers investigating more than 300 land reforms since 1900 found that democracies tend to favor pro-poor and inequality-reducing land reforms (Bhattacharya, Mitra, and Ulubaşoğlu 2019). Governments can, however, find it difficult to undertake land reforms that threaten the interest of the elites. In fact, another global study of land reforms found that since 1945 state expropriation of the property of absentee elites was likely to precipitate regime failure (Hartnett 2018). Even less dramatic reforms remain under discussion indefinitely and fail to be ratified by authorities.

Modernizing land administration is not enough, however. An urgent need is addressing the data gap for improved land governance. Land data are also needed for resilience to shocks (economic, natural, health, conflict) and to facilitate postconflict recovery such as addressing the housing, land, and property rights needs of refugees.

Recent public health crises and violent conflicts have exacerbated the vulnerabilities stemming from weak land rights. The disproportionate impacts on women and vulnerable groups in the form of economic hardships but also more intense tenure insecurity render their inclusion in the land sector even more urgent. These impacts have also brought to light the role that the land sector can play in recovery because leveraging land can offer an opportunity to generate revenue in a context of tight fiscal space.

Finally, the report puts front and center the need for MENA countries to think about land more holistically and to reassess the strategic trade-offs involving land while minimizing land distortions. Four main lessons emerge. First, the scope for land policies needs to be comprehensive, not just sectoral, and take into account market principles and economic and sustainability considerations. Second, trade-offs among issues of food independence, economic efficiency, social equity, and sustainability cannot be avoided, but they should be properly considered in the design of land policies and strategies in the evolving context of climate change, population growth, and the many challenges faced by economies in the region (such as unemployment, gender and economic inequality, and obsolescence of the resource rent model). Third, although the use of land to fulfill the social contract may have laudable social objectives, it has resulted in land inefficiencies and appears to be an inefficient (and unsatisfactory) second-best approach to addressing more fundamental problems of lack of economic redistribution and inclusion. Finally, although progress in land governance is undeniable in some countries and for some aspects of the land sector, there is a need to lay out clear paths for reform and strategies to remove the obstacles that have persistently prevented reform.

REFERENCES

Bhattacharya, P. S., D. Mitra, and M. A. Ulubaşoğlu. 2019. "The Political Economy of Land Reform Enactments: New Cross-National Evidence (1900–2010)." *Journal of Development Economics* 139: 50–68.

Hartnett, A. S. 2018. "Land Reform and Regime Survival in the Middle East and North Africa." Draft prepared for AALIMS-Princeton Conference on the Political Economy of the Muslim World, Princeton University, Princeton, NJ. https://aalims.org/uploads/Hartnett_Land%20Reform%20and%20Regime%20Survival%20 in%20MENA_Aalims.pdf.

www.ingramcontent.com/pod-product-compliance
Lightning Source LLC
Chambersburg PA
CBHW042058210326
41597CB00045B/65